CRAFTSMAN
Bungalows

DESIGNS FROM THE PACIFIC NORTHWEST

YOHO & MERRITT

DOVER PUBLICATIONS, INC.

Mineola, New York

Bibliographical Note

This Dover edition, first published in 2008, is a slightly altered republication of *Craftsman Bungalows, A collection of the latest designs*, originally published by Yoho & Merritt, Seattle, in 1920. A page of advertising testimonials have been omitted from this edition. Please note: The costs of materials and labor cited in this book are out of date and have been included for reference and historic interest.

Library of Congress Cataloging-in-Publication Data

Craftsman bungalows : designs from the Pacific Northwest / Yoho & Merritt. — Dover ed.
    p. cm.
Originally published: Seattle : Yoho & Merritt, 1920.
ISBN-13: 978-0-486-46875-4
ISBN-10: 0-486-46875-5
  1. Bungalows—United States. 2. Small houses—United States. 3. Craftsman Workshops (Eastwood, Syracuse, N.Y.) I. Yoho, Jud, 1882–1968. II. Merritt, Edward L.

NA7571.C75 2008
728'.370973—dc22

                                           2008038517

Manufactured in the United States of America
Dover Publications, Inc., 31 East 2nd Street, Mineola, N.Y. 11501

INTRODUCTION

THE CRAFTSMAN BUNGALOW BOOK is designed to present to those interested in home building the very highest types of bungalows adapted to the cooler climates of the North and East. This book is unique in the fact that while every design or plan shown is a true bungalow, none of them is subject to the handicaps found in the California types, which make no provision for basements, heating plants, and other necessary utilities without which a Northern home is a failure. It is arranged for the purpose of showing, by illustration, floor plans and word descriptions the attractive and comfort-giving features of the Craftsman Bungalow. Many residents of the temperate zone look with envious eyes upon the cozy bungalows of California, while they bemoan the apparent fact that such a type of house would be anything but home-like in cooler climates, with no basement for heating plants or other features of primary importance in a locality where the winters are cold or wet, as in the Northwest and East. To show them that the bungalow type may be adapted to any climate, we have taken the latest designs and arranged the plans for this climate so they will give the greatest degree of satisfaction to the bungalow owner. Realizing some years ago the certain popular demand now being felt for smaller and more convenient houses, we have made a specialty of designing and building these homes in the Northern states and with a success which has been a matter of pride not only to the owners but ourselves as well. Of late other architects have taken up the subject, forced to meet the demand as best they could, whether or not they were familiar with the needs of their sections. They have gone so far in their eagerness to meet all wishes as to apply the term bungalow to many crude alterations of cottages or even more substantial types of residences.

The designing of an artistic bungalow of the true type requires as much skill and education as does any other branch of the architect's work. The man with the experience and training is the one to give you the best results. All of the designs in this book are bungalows pure and simple. Most of them are our own ideas. They are only a few of the many designs on hand, but they will serve to show you something of the concentrated beauty, convenience and comfort to be obtained from owning a real Craftsman Bungalow.

Our estimates of cost, while applying in this city, may be above or below the cost elsewhere, depending on the difference in price of material and labor of all kinds in various parts of the country. Owing to the fluctuations of the labor and material market at the present time it is impossible to prepare estimates which will meet with these conditions at all times. The estimates of cost of construction in this book cover all labor and material complete, with the exception of heating plant, and are based on the following schedule of prices:

COMMON DIMENSION

LUMBER ....$30.00 PER M	FIR LATH..............$ 4.00 PER M	PLASTER ....$20.00 PER TON	MASONRY LABOR $9.00
FINISH LUMBER.......... 70.00 PER M	CEMENT .... 3.25 PER BBL.	CARPENTER LABOR... 7.50	PLUMBING LABOR 9.00
CEDAR SHINGLES...... 4.00 PER M	COMMON BRICK......... 20.00 PER M	COMMON LABOR........ 5.00	PAINTING LABOR 8.00

Labor is all figured on an eight-hour day.

If the exterior and floor plans are suitable, a more or less expensive material may be used to get practically the same results, when the cost figure does not satisfy. A few minor changes in plans can be made to suit individual tastes without changing the outside appearance and without the great expense of re-drawing.

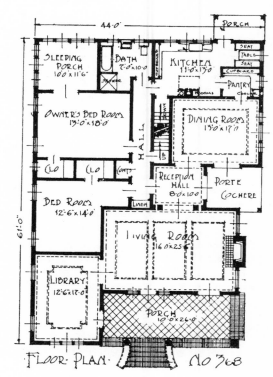

FLOOR PLAN · No 368

368—A veritable mansion and all on one floor, or practically so. The two rooms provided in the rear gable upstairs are small, but amply large enough for the purpose intended. Every room in the house is large and yet not one inch is wasted. Note the convenient arrangement of all rooms—the amount of cupboard space provided in kitchen and pantry. The reception hall is the connecting link between the living room and the balance of the house and serves as an appropriate carriage entrance. The attractive porch is well sheltered and makes a splendid lounge in warm weather. The exterior of the house is sand-finished cement stucco, while the roof is of asphalt shingles curved down at eaves and cornice. The large fluted columns are of wood, while the front steps are paving brick.

Estimated cost...$9600.00
Price of plans as shown or reversed   35.00

Bungalows are here to stay. Their attractiveness and utility assure it.

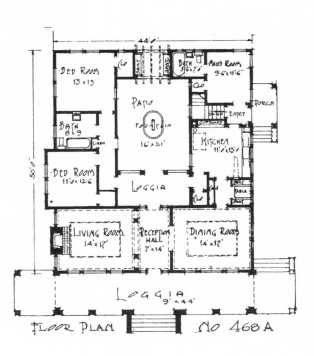

FLOOR PLAN No 468 A

Estimated cost.............................$7500.00

Price of plans as shown or reversed   30.00

468 A—This is one of the best examples of the true Mission style. It has the typical plan of a terrace or "patio" enclosed by three sides of the building. The roof of this house is made of Spanish tile, the exterior is the popular stucco finish over hollow tile. The construction is about as cheap as frame in many parts of the country, and in the long run costs less, if the job is done right. The principal rooms are finished with cove ceilings and hardwood floors. The living room fireplace is very large and of beautiful design. The plans provide for large, well-arranged rooms, large closets and all modern conveniences, including a built-in pullman diner and ironing board in kitchen. The glassed in Loggia is so arranged that it can be used as a summer dining room overlooking the patio with its flowers and tumbling fountain.

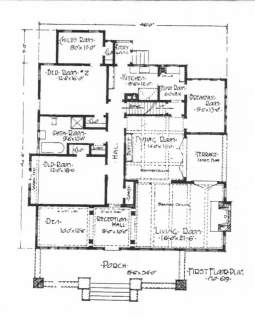

619—An exterior which is practically a duplicate of that shown on page seven and a plan arrangement that is very similar but on a slightly larger scale. Two rooms—namely, den and child's room—are provided in this plan which are not to be found in plan number 467, and by the provision of a few more windows the child's room could very easily be used as a sleeping porch if so desired. A glance at the living room interior shown on this page will give one an idea of the splendid opportunity offered in the fine large rooms. The difference of six feet in width between this home and its prototype has certainly been used to advantage as can be readily seen in a comparison of bedrooms. The attic plan calls for a division of the space into two bedrooms, sleeping porch and generous closets.

Estimated cost.....................................$6600.00

Price of plans as shown or reversed   20.00

Our plans are revelations in the utilization of space.

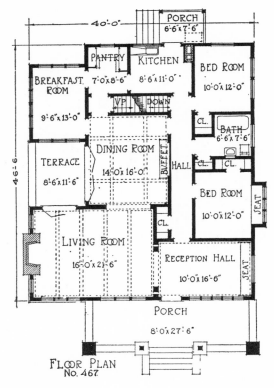

FLOOR PLAN No. 467

- PORCH 6'-6" x 7'-6"
- PANTRY 7'-0" x 8'-6"
- KITCHEN 8'-6" x 11'-0"
- BED ROOM 10'-0" x 12'-0"
- BREAKFAST ROOM 9'-6" x 13'-0"
- UP / DOWN
- CL.
- BATH 6'-6" x 7'-6"
- DINING ROOM 14'-0" x 16'-0"
- BUFFET
- HALL
- TERRACE 8'-6" x 11'-6"
- CL. CL.
- BED ROOM 10'-0" x 12'-0"
- SEAT
- LIVING ROOM 16'-0" x 21'-6"
- CL.
- RECEPTION HALL 10'-0" x 16'-6"
- SEAT
- PORCH 8'-0" x 27'-6"
- 40'-0"
- 46'-6"

Estimated cost..................................$6400.00
Price of plans as shown or reversed   20.00

467—This is a style of bungalow that is becoming very popular in the Western states. The lines of the house are very graceful and the whole effect is very attractive. The design calls for brick veneer to the height of the watertable with sawed shakes above. The brick-faced porch and chimney give the building a substantial air of plenty, borne out by the very liberal lines of the house. The living and dining rooms are connected by a wide opening, which may, if desired, convert them into practically one room. There are two bed rooms with small halls, each with a door leading to either the kitchen or bath room. Perhaps the most attractive feature of this design is the large breakfast room, which opens from the pantry and dining room and so arranged that it has windows on three sides.

Our plans are practical.

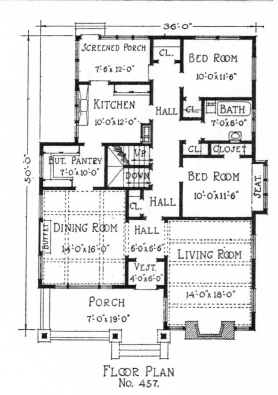

FLOOR PLAN
No. 457.

457—It is hard to keep from getting enthusiastic about as pretty a bungalow as this, especially after an inspection of the house itself. "Solid and sensible" just describe it. Where large rooms and closet space are needed, it would be hard to find a nicer plan than this. The entrance is into a vestibule which opens into a reception hall with living and dining rooms on opposite sides. The porch floor is cement on dirt filling. The house is very well planned with all the rooms independent of each other, yet easy of access. The dining room has an exceptionally fine buffet. The living room is large and has a large open fireplace.

Estimated cost...........................$6000.00

Price of plans as shown or reversed   20.00

The fireplace is the center of the home—build it right.

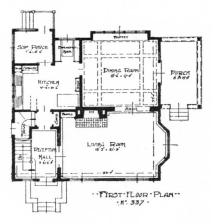

FIRST·FLOOR·PLAN
·Nº 337·

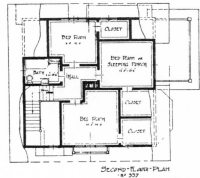

SECOND·FLOOR·PLAN
·Nº 337·

Estimated cost.............................$6000.00
Price of plans as shown or reversed 20.00

337—A story and a half house of very pleasing proportions and carefully thought out, different detail. Note the extra wide verge boards and rich, heavy moldings. The first story is shingles in alternate courses. The second story is cement plaster on galvanized metal lath. The curved hood over the front entrance and the balcony effect of the second story windows break up an otherwise rather plain wall. Three large, well planned rooms are provided on the first floor, with splendid outlook on all sides. The upper floor, reached from the reception hall, has fine bedrooms and another room which can be used either as a bedroom or sleeping porch. The bathroom is placed where it is handy to all rooms, as well as economical for plumbing. The house proper is 33' 0" wide and 33' 0" deep.

322—A CREDITABLE EXAMPLE OF THE CEMENT PLASTERED RESIDENCE

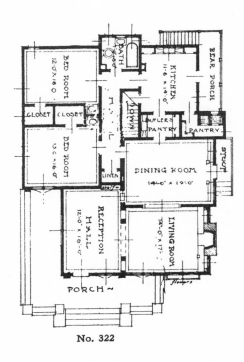

No. 322

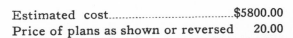

Estimated cost..$5800.00

Price of plans as shown or reversed   20.00

322—While varying somewhat from what one would ordinarily term bungalow, this design has several points of merit. The light and cheerful aspect of the cement plaster forms a pleasing contrast with the dark red brick pilasters. The house is very conveniently arranged, and each bed room is provided with a clothes closet and lavatory. Access is had to the bath room through a hall, which is lighted and ventilated by a skylight. The dining room is paneled to a height of the plate rail, above which in square forms extend quaint Dutch figures around the room.

Be not the first by whom the new was tried, nor yet the last to lay the old aside.

327—HALF TIMBER AND GRANITE—A FINE BUNGALOW OF LARGE CAPACITY

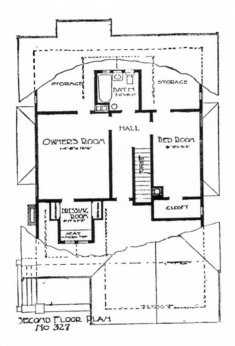

SECOND FLOOR PLAN No 327

Estimated cost.................................$5700.00

Price of plans as shown or reversed   20.00

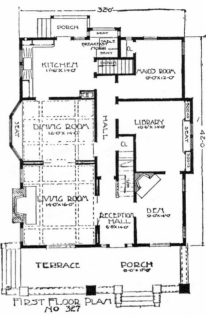

FIRST FLOOR PLAN No 327

327—This eight-room bungalow is of a type which we may call medium cost and large accommodation. The design savors of great substantiality, notably in the foundation walls and the granite rubble of the porch work and chimneys. The little note of half timber which shines in gables is a very pretty note. The disposition of the various rooms is good, and a room, the library, is provided which can be used as a bed room if the size of the family necessitates. Upstairs are two large bed rooms, each having its own light and roomy closet, the bath room and storage space under the eaves.

634—THE AEROPLANE TYPE

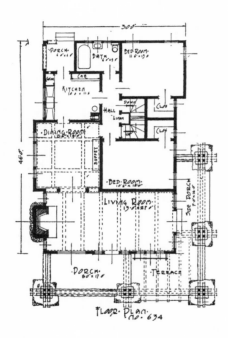

FLOOR-PLAN·No·634·

Estimated cost.........................$5500.00
Price of plans as shown or reversed   20.00

634—In design this is a good example of that known on the Pacific Coast as the aeroplane type, and its style of architectural treatment, its many curved rafters, ridges and brackets is derived from the architecture of Japan and China. The "curve" idea has been carried out very consistently and just far enough, as a study of the exterior will convince. The cobblestone work in this house is of the very best. In plan this is one of the best arrangements for five rooms. A splendid living room opening to two porches, the side porch being in reality a carriage entrance, a dining room, kitchen, two bed rooms and bath. Note the large closets and the way the stairs have been schemed to take up as little room as possible. The second story, which we are unable to show for lack of room, has one bed room or dressing room, and a large sleeping porch open on three sides.

"One need not necessarily be rich to give grace and charm to his habitation."—Wagner.

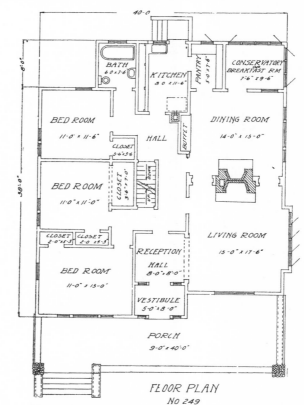

FLOOR PLAN
NO 249

249—Elaborate both as to the outside and inside design, this bungalow will attract the better class of house owners not only by its pretentious appearance but by the features of the interior, which include a cozy vestibule and reception hall, fireplace in both living and dining rooms, a buffet in the last named room, and, best of all, a breakfast room practically enclosed in glass, available to the kitchen with the same easy access as the dining room. The exterior of the house employs cobblestones and brick on the front with artistic effect, while the dark woodwork with its lighter trimmings makes a pleasing background for the house. The reception hall leads into the commodious living room, which practically extends from the front of the house to the breakfast room in the rear, with a huge fireplace exactly in the center.

Estimated cost.....................................$5300.00
Price of plans as shown or reversed   15.00

FLOOR PLAN No. 419.

Estimated cost..................................$5300.00

Price of plans as shown or reversed   15.00

419—This is one of the extreme type of bungalows, and wherever built it cannot help but attract a great deal of favorable comment. The very exterior of the house spells comfort. The use of cobblestones of assorted size and color for the fireplace and porch walls adds a pleasing touch to the exterior. The interior is about as conveniently arranged as is possible to plan a bungalow. Every room has a clothes closet and a pass hall connecting with the bath. The dining room has beam ceilings and paneled wainscoting. The plumbing in this house is especially well arranged; in being grouped together it can be installed at a smaller cost than is general in bungalows.

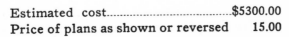

Bed room windows should give light to your dressing table.

357—A one and one-half story home of unusual merit. Five splendid rooms and sleeping porch of good size, containing all the latest conveniences, in the way of built-in features. Note the practical arrangement of breakfast nook, ironing board and cabinets; also the buffet and inviting fireplace. The downstairs hall will save steps. Fine roomy closets are provided in abundance. The open balcony makes a comportable upstairs porch. The basement, under the entire house, is fitted up for laundry, furnace and fuel rooms and fruit storage. Four-inch cedar siding as the exterior wall covering lends a distinctive appearance to this attractive home.

Estimated cost.....................................$5300.00
Price of plans as shown or reversed   15.00

Our plans include details of interior finish.

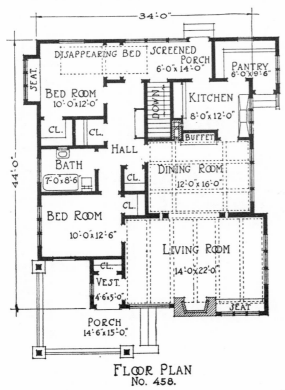

FLOOR PLAN
No. 458.

Estimated cost...................................$5200.00

Price of plans as shown or reversed   15.00

458—Departing somewhat from the exterior appearance of the conventional five-room bungalow is this pretty home. Perhaps the most attractive feature of this plan is the bed room, equipped with a reversible concealed bed, so arranged that it can be used either in the bed room or in the sleeping porch in the rear. The living room is unusually large and is divided from the dining room by an open arch. Both of the principal rooms have beam ceilings and paneled wainscoting. Although the kitchen is small, ample cupboard space is provided in the pantry. The plan affords a great deal more closet space than is generally found in a bungalow. Special notice is called to the convenient way in which the rooms are grouped around the pass hall.

323—A POPULAR DESIGN OF CEMENT PLASTERED BUNGALOW

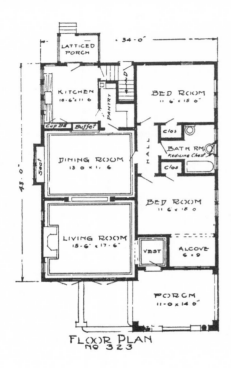

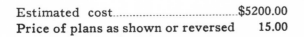

FLOOR PLAN
NO 323

323—We show here a very popular design for a cement plaster bungalow, roofed with imitation Spanish tile made from galvanized sheet iron. While the first cost of such a roof is somewhat higher than shingles, when one considers the saving in the continual upkeep of expense of a shingle roof the ultimate cost of a more permanent material will be seen to be no higher. The rooms are larger than are ordinarily found in a bungalow and are arranged for convenience.

Estimated cost.................................$5200.00
Price of plans as shown or reversed 15.00

He that has a bungalow to put his head in, has a good headpiece.

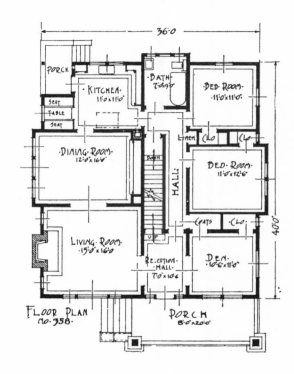

FLOOR PLAN
No. 358.

358—A large house attractively designed for a corner lot. Thirty-six by forty feet in its over-all dimensions, this house requires a lot at least sixty feet in width to set it off properly. Six fine rooms on the first floor, arranged so that the den can be used as a bed room if required, with access to hall through coat closet, without entering the reception hall. The hall connects all rooms, doing away with the necessity of disturbing your guests in living room or dining room when answering the front door bell. French doors are hung at all wide openings to living room, dining room and den; and the door from reception hall to rear hall is also a glass door. An immense buffet is provided in dining room against the inside wall. Several additional rooms can be placed on the second floor.

Estimated cost.................................$5000.00
Price of plans as shown or reversed   15.00

A wise builder buys good plans.

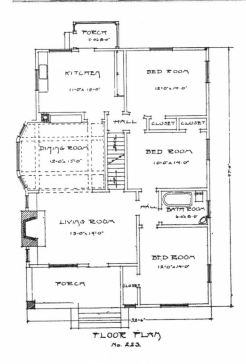

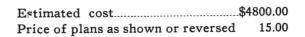

FLOOR PLAN
No. 223.

PORCH
KITCHEN
11'-0" x 15'-0"
BED ROOM
12'-0" x 14'-0"
HALL
CLOSET CLOSET
DINING ROOM
12'-0" x 15'-0"
BED ROOM
10'-0" x 14'-0"
HALL
BATH ROOM
6'-0" x 8'-0"
LIVING ROOM
13'-0" x 19'-0"
BED ROOM
12'-0" x 14'-0"
PORCH
CLOSET

Estimated cost.........................$4800.00
Price of plans as shown or reversed   15.00

223—This is a roomy house with no ginger-bread effects, yet altogether a pleasing shingled exterior. Two outside closets, three bed rooms, with another room available upstairs, show something of the excellent manner in which the bungalow is designed. The brick-faced porch and chimney give the place a substantial air of plenty, borne out by the liberal lines of the house. The living and dining rooms are connected by a wide opening which may, if desired, convert the two into practically one room. The cellar stairs are beneath the flight leading to the upper floor. Perhaps the most attractive room of the house is the dining room, large and cheerful with its huge bay window, its heavy beam ceiling and cozy buffet niche, which gives additional space for table and chairs.

Our plans are a little better than seems necessary.

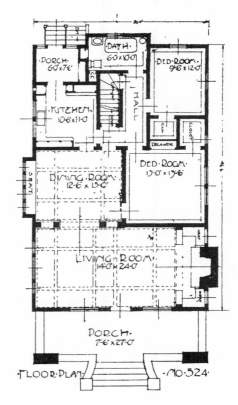

524—Another extremely popular design of five rooms on the ground floor with two bed rooms, one 14 by 14 feet, the other 10 feet 6 inches by 14 feet, and sleeping porch of ample size on the second floor. The fireplace is enclosed in an ingle nook with seats on either side. Large, roomy closets are provided for all the bed rooms and the bath room is located convenient to all rooms. The plan calls for a brick flue in the kitchen for kitchen range and laundry stove. The furnace flue is in the fireplace chimney.

Estimated cost...$4800.00

Price of plans as shown or reversed   15.00

Convenience in our plans is our main object.

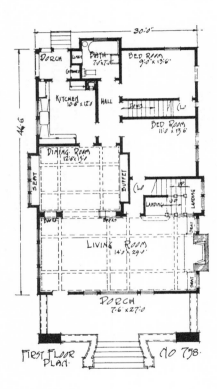

758—This home, the plan on the left, designed to fit the exterior shown on page twenty, gives the same number of rooms in practically the same plan with one essential change, namely, that of providing for a stairway to the second floor in the front of the house. Other changes are the elimination of ingle nook in front of fireplace and the addition of an immense buffet to the built-in features of the house. The second floor provides two bed rooms and a sleeping porch. The outside wall covering is cement stucco.

351—Another plan for the same house, only on a much smaller scale, calling only for the five rooms on the main floor in a ground space 24 by 40. We have kept all the main features of the original house and have shown a plan that will become very popular. Note the neat "Pullman diner" provided. If one desires a still less expensive home on this type, they are referred to number 747 on page 92.

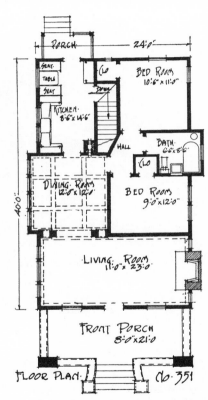

Estimated cost................................$4800.00
Price of plans as shown or reversed   15.00

Estimated cost................................$3300.00
Price of plans as shown or reversed   15.00

Our designs are combinations of art, science and sentiment.

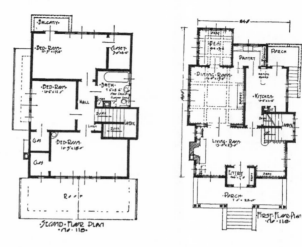

118—This seven-room home is twenty-four feet by forty feet on the ground. By the clever use of several very ordinary materials, each in its proper place and broad horizontal lines, an appearance of breadth is given which is further enhanced by the many roofs, every one legitimate. The basement walls to a watertable placed at the window sill of the first floor are covered with four-inch cedar siding. Above this are shingles laid four inches to the weather. The gables are of pebble dashed cement stucco, paneled with narrow wood strips. The seven rooms are well placed. The four living rooms are closely connected on the first floor, while the three bedrooms are grouped about the bathroom hall on the second floor. Large closets are provided for all rooms and two linen closets are also provided.

Estimated cost..............................$4800.00

Price of plans as shown or reversed   15.00

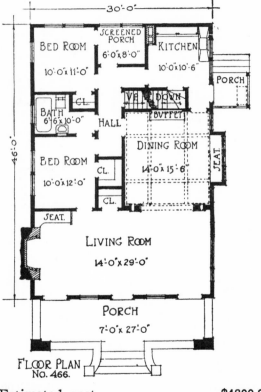

FLOOR PLAN
No. 466.

Estimated cost $4800.00
Price of plans as shown or reversed   15.00

466—One test of the popularity of a bungalow is the number of people who have built in a similar style   In our city it is built with many variations in the detail of interior arrangement.   The porch is of course the original and attractive feature of this bungalow. If properly constructed, the gable on the roof is a great success, but the plans must be followed very carefully.   Although the ceiling in the second story is low, ample room is provided for two small chambers and a sleeping porch.   The exterior is sided with sawed cedar shakes laid 12 inches to the weather and stained a dark gray, which forms a striking contrast to the white trim of the smooth woodwork.   This is one of our very best houses.

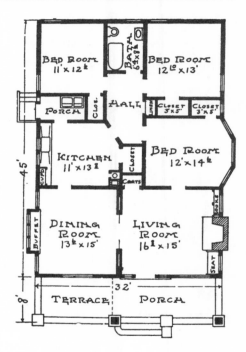

300—With attractive double gables and striking contrast of stone terrace and shingled exterior, this is a typical southern bungalow, adapted to cold climatic conditions. It is a genuine surprise as to size, having six large, well-arranged rooms with not a foot of waste space. The fireplace, flanked by book shelves and window seat, is an ornament both within and without, its outside brick chimney affording an ideal footing for climbing vines. The terrace of dressed stone must be seen to be appreciated fully. A fine idea, that of having the laundry trays on the enclosed back porch. The closet space is extended rather than cramped by this porch. Think of it, a closet for every room. There are four large and two small closets, one for coats and hats off the living room and for linen off the hall leading into the bath room.

Estimated cost $3,800.00
Price of plans as shown or reversed   15.00

Do not assume—be sure you are right—get our plans.

PAGE TWENTY-EIGHT

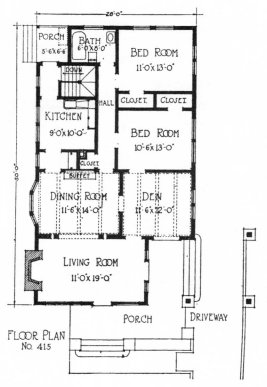

FLOOR PLAN No. 415

Rooms labeled: PORCH 5'-6"x6'-6", BATH 6'-0"x8'-0", BED ROOM 11'-0"x13'-0", KITCHEN 9'-0"x10'-0", HALL, CLOSET, CLOSET, BED ROOM 10'-6"x13'-0", BUFFET, DINING ROOM 11'-6"x14'-0", DEN 11'-6"x12'-0", LIVING ROOM 11'-0"x19'-0", PORCH, DRIVEWAY, CLOSET, DOWN

Estimated cost.................................$4800.00
Price of plans as shown or reversed   15.00

415—This small and attractive home has been very popular everywhere. The photograph fails to do justice to its real beauty. The outside is a combination of the rustic siding and clinker brick. The house being on the more extreme bungalow order, finds especial favor in communities building the cottage style of houses. A more convenient plan can not be found. The buffet in the dining room is larger than in most small houses, being five feet wide. The fireplace is of pressed brick with a cut stone shelf. A kitchen cabinet is designed complete, having doors and drawers below the counter shelf and a cupboard above built to the ceiling. There is a cement basement in this house, with a stairway opening from the rear porch.

Interior Design 312—This interior shows the use which can be made of beam ceilings. Both the living and dining rooms are beamed, while a wainscoting of wood may be employed with great effectiveness for the walls of the former. The entrance to the dining room, with its short, square columns and high paneling, is very attractive. The sandstone fireplace, with ledge of stone for mantel shelf and stained glass windows on either side, makes a very pleasing contrast to the dark woodwork so prominent in the room.

Interior Design 412—A simple but attractive interior, showing the use of square tile for the mantel. The interior woodwork is square design, and the whole is finished in a dark brown with light cream ceilings. The stained art glass used in the high windows on either side of the fireplace lends the touch of color needed to make the whole a most pleasing effect. The walls of this living room are tinted a deep tan, while the ceiling is a light cream tone. The dining room, a glimpse of which is had through the arch, is paneled five feet six inches high with slash grain fir panels capped with a plate rail.

A cooling cabinet can be arranged in almost any kitchen.

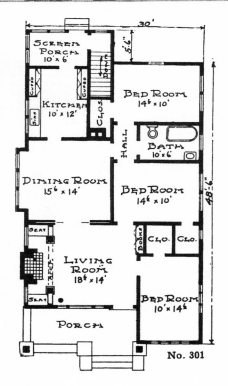

No. 301

Estimated cost.............................$4800.00

Price of plans as shown or reversed   15.00

301—Overhanging eaves, a wide verge board, with heavy exposed braces and casement windows make the exterior of this bungalow unique and cozy in appearance. The stone porch leading to the heavy mission door with its great hinges, sets off the dark rustic woodwork. The ingle nook in the large living room is the most striking feature of the structure. With wide leather seats on either side and at right angles to the old English fireplace, the mantel of pressed brick and the sunken hearth, all unite to give charm to the little room separated by a graceful arch from the living room and forming a lounging den for men, women or children which cannot be excelled. The screen porch at the rear is a feature which holds the wife as the smoking nook does the husband. The kitchen is designed purely for business purposes and to save steps. The porch may be used for a store room or annex and in summer for a breakfast room.

The planning of a bungalow home is an art.

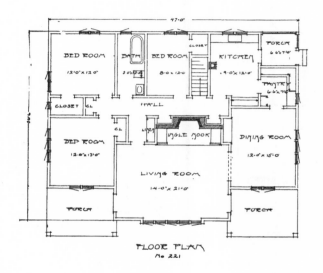

FLOOR PLAN
No. 221

221—Unpretentious in exterior appearance, this bungalow contains a multitude of special features that cannot fail to win approval on every hand. The living room opens on both porches, one railed in with a rustic fence and the other open to the street. The mantel is wide and at either side are broad, inviting seats, forming a partial enclosure in which the family and guests may gather and toast marshmallows or pop corn of a winter's evening. The dining room is provided with casement windows and the pair opening out onto the porch may if desired be French windows, serving as doors at need. There is a neat pass pantry leading to the kitchen, off which latter room a porch abuts. A hall leads from the kitchen to the three bed rooms and living room, with openings for linen and coat closets, for the cellar stairs and into the bath room.

Estimated cost $4800.00
Price of plans as shown or reversed   15.00

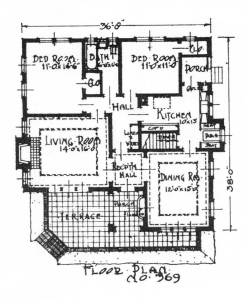

FLOOR PLAN No. 369

369—A splendid adaptation of the old English, thatched roof farm house, but constructed of much more substantial materials. The stucco is rough cast on hollow tile and the roof is asbestos shingles. Can you imagine anything better in the way of building materials? Hollow tile is one of the most fireproof building materials ever put on the market, while asbestos is the one word first thought of when thinking of fire prevention. Think of it; you will never have to paint your walls and the roof never requires any stain but remains the same color to the end of time. This is not a large house and can easily be built on a fifty-foot lot and leave ample room for driveway and garage. The interior arrangement is well worthy of its exterior—Every possible convenience is provided and an extremely practical plan has been evolved—one which means careful study.

Estimated cost.................................$4800.00
Price of plans as shown or reversed   15.00

J·UD·YOHO
ARCHITECT

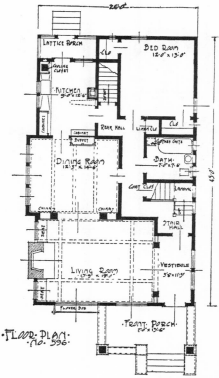

·FLOOR· PLAN·
·No· 596·

596—The story and a half of the elevation has lent itself to a very pleasing treatment. With alternate coursed shingles, stained silver gray, white painted trim and the red burlap texture of the brick, we have a combination that is hard to beat. The flaring skirting below the heavy watertable relieves a design which otherwise might by some be considered too severe. In this plan we have the sleeping quarters entirely separated from the living room and by the same token have made it possible for one to go from front to rear of house or upstairs, without passing through any of the rooms. Upstairs we have sufficient space for one large bedroom, a smaller one and a sleeping porch.

Estimated cost................................$4700.00
Price of plans as shown or reversed   15.00

"No single parts unequally surprise, all come united to admiring eyes."

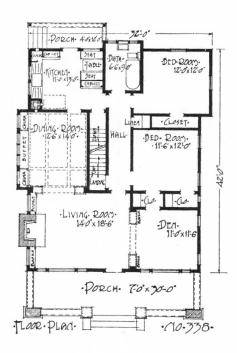

·FLOOR·PLAN· · NO. 338 ·

Estimated cost..$4700.00
Price of plans as shown or reversed   15.00

338—Unfortunately our photographer was unable, owing to local conditions, to show the attractive side of this bungalow, but with the assistance of the floor plan, one can readily see a pretty design. The rather large expanse of plain roof is relieved by a gable dormer, just large enough to look right, and provide enough light in the attic. The little touch of vertical boarding in the side gables, sets off the simplicity of the shingled walls. The porch walls and piers are red paving brick laid up in colored mortar. The floor plan arrangement is very good, calling for six fine rooms of splendid size and every imaginable built-in feature; bookcases, china closets, buffet, ample cabinet space in kitchen, and last but not least, the neat Pullman diner. Properly set off by shrubbery and lawn, this bungalow makes an artistic home in any neighborhood.

Bungalows are here to stay. Their attractiveness and utility assure it.

PAGE THIRTY-FIVE

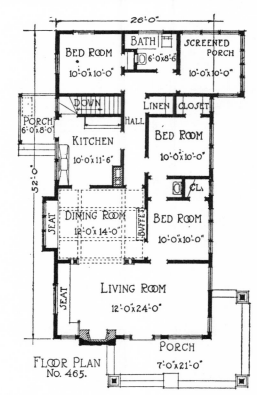

FLOOR PLAN
No. 465.

465—This is certainly a most pleasing design and is a characteristic Craftsman bungalow. The cobblestones used in the porch pedestals and fireplace are very artistic. The plan of the house answers all the requirements of the average small family and includes a large open air sleeping porch that could be finished as a bed room if desired. The buffet in the dining room is larger than in most bungalows, being five feet wide. It contains deep drawers and cupboards for the accommodation of a large quantity of china and linen. The fireplace mantel is of cut stone and is very massive in appearance. The large window in the living room is plate glass. A New Jersey man who secured the plans of this house describes it as the most aristocratic little home he ever saw.

Estimated cost...$4700.00
Price of plans as shown or reversed   15.00

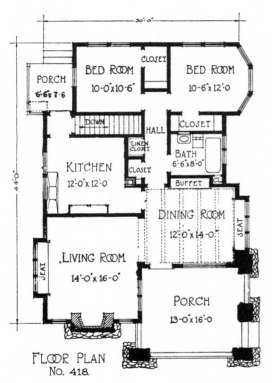

FLOOR PLAN NO. 418

Estimated cost.................................$4600.00

Price of plans as shown or reversed   15.00

418—This bungalow is a perfect example of bungalow architecture, and has proved to be one of the most popular styles ever designed. The unique feature of the exterior is the introduction of cobblestones for the massive porch columns. The well-proportioned roof and wide overhanging eaves lend an individuality to this design that has met with favor in every part of the United States. The shingles are laid in alternate courses and stained a golden brown to complete the scheme. The principal rooms of this house are models of convenience and comfort. The dining room has beam ceiling and panel walls, with a large built-in buffet. The bed room arrangement is good and affords ample closet space.

We render the best architectural service.

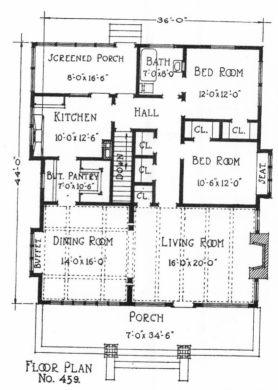

FLOOR PLAN No. 459.

459—The light and cheerful aspect of this bungalow appeals to old and young couples alike. There is a cosy old-fashionedness about the exterior that catches the more sedate, while the wealth of light and sunshine from the multitude of windows unite to make the interior most pleasing and attractive. It is a cheerful little house with a homey arrangement and porch effects. The rough sawed cedar shakes and casement windows and other bungalow features are here prominent. Concrete blocks are here used for porch pedestals and the steps are cement. The rear porch is of ample size and can be used as a breakfast room if so desired on warm summer days.

Estimated cost................................$4600.00
Price of plans as shown or reversed   15.00

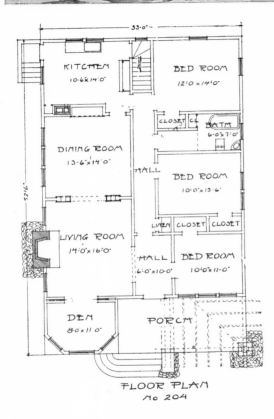

FLOOR PLAN
No 204

Estimated cost..................................$4600.00

Price of plans as shown or reversed   15.00

Have the housewife's workshop complete (it improves the cooking).

204—A cobblestone chimney and porch pillar combine with the pergola on one side and bay window on the other to give this bungalow a cozy, yet distinctive appearance. The den with its broad seat in the bay window is an ideal place for a lounging or rest room. The living room fire is in view and the wide entrance to the dining room helps to extend the vista to the buffet 35 feet away. There are three bed rooms in this house, all opening into the hall leading to the large bath room. The closet provision for the house will impress the wife at once. There is a towel closet in the bath room, one for linen in the hall, three for clothes in the bed rooms and a broom closet in the kitchen. The interior is well planned, and it is the utilization of every inch of space for some handy purpose that makes this and other bungalows so popular as homes.

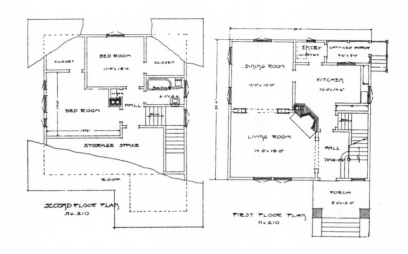

210—A two-story house whose exposed rafters, wide eaves, rustic siding and clinker brick porch supports and columns give it the bungalow air, is shown here for the family which prefers the sleeping rooms on the second floor. The exterior trim includes caps over the windows and a ledge extending across the full width of the porch. The entry hall has an attractive staircase and landing leading to the second floor. A passageway takes one directly into the kitchen if desired. A wide opening with a charming arch connects living and dining rooms, permitting the warmth of the corner fireplace to permeate both. The bath and bed rooms are on the second floor, the stairs ending in a hallway on which these rooms all open. There is opportunity to make a private servant's room of the storage space under the front eaves by cutting in a skylight or installing a dormer window.

Estimated cost.....................................$4600.00
Price of plans as shown or reversed   15.00

Bed room windows should give light to your dressing table.

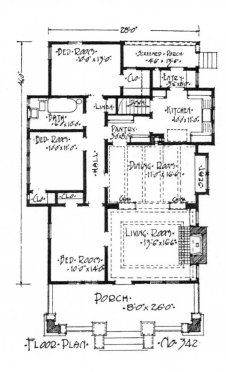

342—This beautiful design is a sister to the most popular house in America, and while differing from her sister in some essential properties, has many advantages in her own name that well repay careful consideration. The porch piers and buttresses are finished with sand sprayed cement stucco. The house is sheathed with wide and narrow boards of rough siding. The porch floor is cement. Parts of the exterior that are worthy of study are the attractively different window casings, the unique gable trim and the cut of the Swiss brackets. The plan calls for six fine rooms with numerous closets. The three bedrooms are all closely connected by the hall, off which are the dining room and pantry as well as the bath room. More than the usual amount of cabinet space is provided and the cooling cabinet and refrigerator are given space in the rear entry.

Estimated cost...$4500.00
Price of plans as shown or reversed   15.00

324—VERY PLEASING AND INVITING

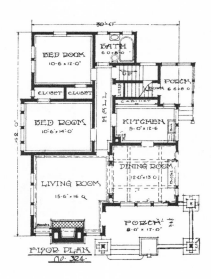

FLOOR PLAN
NO. 324

324—This bungalow makes a very pleasing and inviting home in every respect. The fireplace and porch columns are stucco finish. Every room in the house is of good proportion and there is every desirable convenience. The screened porch is of good size. A little hallway between the bed rooms is a good feature, giving entrance from any part of the house to the bath. In every way we recommend this as one of our most desirable bungalows. There is ample room on the second floor for a couple of small chambers, as well as a sleeping porch in the rear.

Estimated cost............................$4400.00
Price of plans as shown or reversed   15.00

He that has a bungalow to put his head in, has a good headpiece.

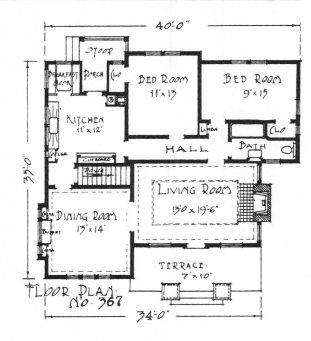

FLOOR PLAN No. 367

367—A wonderful home in a wonderful setting. May your choice be as good. The surroundings can make or mar the passer's-by first impression and too much thought cannot be given in laying out the grounds. This splendid design certainly earns the admiration which has been bestowed upon it. The exterior of narrow cedar lap-siding painted white, forms a pleasing background for trellised vines; and the iron-barred windows lend a touch of mystery to an otherwise ordinary combination of materials. Ready-roofing makes a fine water-tight roof for low pitches such as this, and if a good brand is selected will give no trouble and will last for many years. The different rooms are well arranged and labor-saving conveniences add to the attractiveness of the different rooms.

Estimated cost $4400.00
Price of plans as shown or reversed   15.00

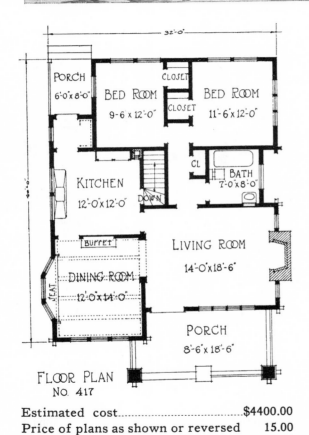

FLOOR PLAN
NO. 417

Estimated cost..................................$4400.00
Price of plans as shown or reversed   15.00

417—The photograph speaks for the attractiveness of the exterior and the plan suggests how cozy and comfortable the interior may be made. The fireplace and porch columns are stucco finish; the outside is cedar shingles. The closets are all large. Every room of the house is of good proportion and there is every desirable convenience. The linen closet in the pass hall has a clothes chute leading to the basement. The basement occupies the space under the bed room, bath and kitchen, and is floored with concrete. This is a very desirable home for any locality.

Don't let over-confidence in your own ability spoil your bungalow.

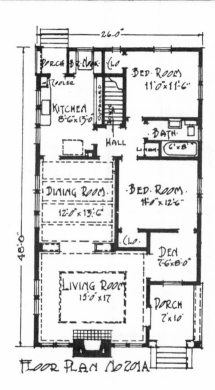

FLOOR PLAN No 201 A

201 A—Six rooms and bath. The sixth, the Den, so named, is ideally located for any number of uses: a child's room, office, sewing room, as well as a cozy den. Entrance is made directly into the large living room from the side porch. The cheery, inviting fireplace is to the left, while farther to the right is the arched opening to the dining room. The living room has a cove and ceiling panel mold, while the dining room calls for beam ceiling and wood-panellel walls, enamelled white or stained as the case may be. The little interior hall connects most of the rooms with the bath and from this hall the stairs lead to the basement. Eight-six by thirteen in this plan means an ideal kitchen with plenty of roomy cupboard space and cooler, and also finding room for one of the prettiest of breakfast nooks. The exterior of shingles, six inches to the weather, is dominated by the large stucco chimney.

Estimated cost..................................$4300.00
Price of plans as shown or reversed   15.00

Our designs are combinations of art, science and sentiment.

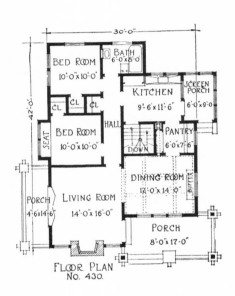

FLOOR PLAN No. 430.

430—An extremely popular style of building in all parts of the West. It makes a very pleasing and inviting home in every respect. The porch is eight by seventeen feet with heavy cement columns in battered forms. The living room with its low French windows opening on to the terrace is one of the attractive features of this design. The kitchen and pantry are models of convenience and contain all the necessities. The screen porch is of good size. A little hallway between the bed rooms is a good feature, giving entrance from any part of the house to the bath. In every way, we recommend this as one of our most desirable bungalows.

Estimated cost...$4300.00
Price of plans as shown or reversed   15.00

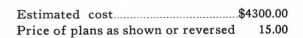

Save yourself time and worry by purchasing our plans.

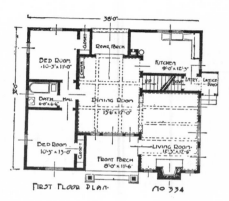

FIRST FLOOR PLAN.   NO 334

334—This bungalow requires a lot at least 50 feet wide. It will be noticed that exclusive of the porches the house is 38 feet wide and only 32 feet deep. The design calls plainly for a rough texture and for light colors. The shingled walls are stained silver gray, the trim, including sash, is painted white and the roof a light green or brown. There are five large rooms on the first floor and sufficient height in the attic for two rooms and the sleeping porch.

Estimated cost..$4200.00
Price of plans as shown or reversed   15.00

While we make a specialty of bungalows, we also design two-story houses—Write us.

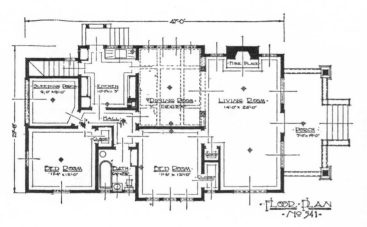

Estimated cost................................$4200.00

Price of plans as shown or reversed   15.00

541—A very practical design of five rooms.   The full width of the living room is fourteen feet, and it reaches from one side wall to the other.   The dining room has beamed ceiling and paneled wainscot.   A sleeping porch is included in the plan connected to either of the bed rooms by the hall.   The kitchen is of the cabinet pattern; everything used in the kitchen may be kept out of sight here and kept spotlessly clean.

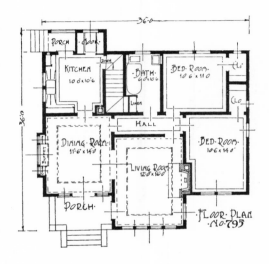

795—An up-to-date modern and attractive five-room cottage-bungalow. We use this term to identify this style of home from what we come to know as the original bungalow of the Pacific Coast, that of wide-spreading eaves and expansive roof; and the newer semi and strictly Colonial types illustrated elsewhere in this volume. Seven-Ninety-Five partakes of the characteristics of both types, and is a home that has a style all its own. The water table placed at the sill line and the horizontal line of the eaves tend to lower the house in the mind of the passerby, without doing so in actual fact. The roof shingles are laid with every fifth course doubled, which helps to relieve the otherwise plain surface. The five rooms are of good size and very conveniently arranged.

Estimated cost................................$4100.00

Price of plans as shown or reversed   15.00

We render the best architectural service.

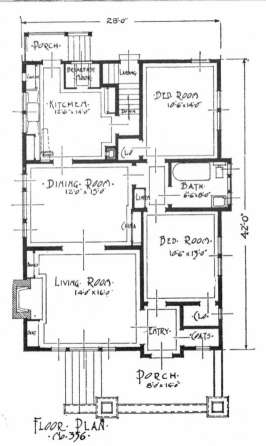

FLOOR PLAN No. 356

- PORCH
- BREAKFAST NOOK
- LANDING
- KITCHEN 12'6" x 14'0"
- DOWN
- BED ROOM 10'6" x 14'0"
- DINING ROOM 12'0" x 15'0"
- BATH 6'6" x 8'0"
- LINEN
- CHINA
- BED ROOM 10'6" x 13'0"
- LIVING ROOM 14'0" x 16'0"
- ENTRY
- COATS
- SEAT
- PORCH 8'0" x 16'0"
- 28'-0"
- 42'-0"

356—Five rooms and bath, with entrance hall, fireplace and breakfast nook, besides all the other built-in conveniences our clients have come to expect. This plan is to satisfy a long list of would-be home builders who are still looking for the "one-and-only." Note the sizes of the different rooms and the roomy cabinet space provided in kitchen, the china closet in dining room, and linen cabinet in hall designed to contain a clothes chute to basement. The exterior combines several materials and finishes. The porch walls and piers are of burlap, or as it is known in the East, tapestry brick. The skirting of the house is of wide and narrow rough siding alternate, stained. Above the water-table we find four-inch smooth siding painted; and the gables are finished with shingles, alternate wide and narrow courses, and stained a golden brown.

Estimated cost........$4100.00   Price of plans as shown or reversed   15.00

The design and not the amount of lumber draws forth the favorable comment.

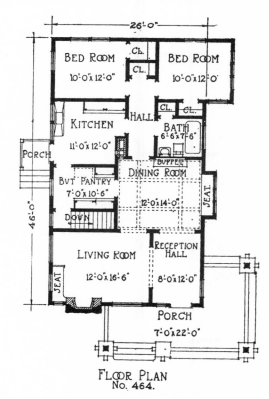

FLOOR PLAN
No. 464.

464—A good substantial bungalow of the Craftsman type with every requisite for comfort. It has very pretty exterior lines, broken artistically by heavy exposed rafter ends and large brackets; a good roomy porch with cobblestone foundation and pillars. Clinker brick may be used if desired. The roofing is ready-prepared roofing, colored with fine white sand, and is warranted by manufacturers. The floor plan is self-explanatory. Note the open fireplace with cosy seat on the side; the buffet in dining room; the handy kitchen and pass pantry; convenient bath room, etc. The closet space allowed will be a delight to the tidy housewife. The large reception hall is a good feature.

Estimated cost..$4100.00

Price of plans as shown or reversed   15.00

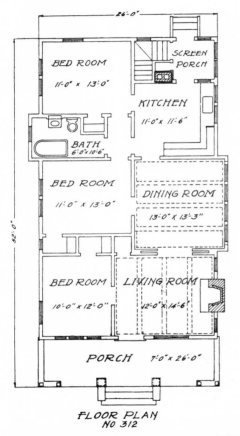

FLOOR PLAN
NO 312

Price of plans as shown or reversed 15.00
Estimated cost....$4100.00

312—An attractive design worthy to be set upon a hill is this home of six rooms. Resawed siding with vari-colored brick for the large chimney, cream or white trimmings on a dark background of roof and house give the most effective appearance. The porch, protected by the gable roof, extends across the entire width of the house. The kitchen has a large screen porch adjoining, with stairway leading to the cellar. The bed room arrangement is unique, but eminently satisfactory. A small hall gives access to dining room, kitchen and two bed rooms. The third bed room may be used as a library or den, or if preferred, the removal of the partition will convert the living room into a great hall 24 feet long and 12 feet wide.

Have the housewife's workshop complete (it improves the cooking).

Estimated cost....$4000.00

Price of plans as shown
or reversed $15.00

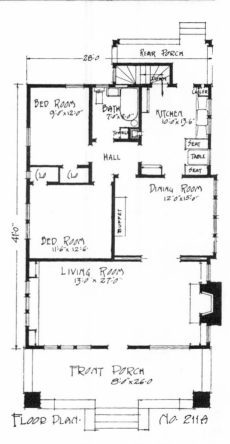

FLOOR PLAN. No. 211A

211-A—Rustic siding and cobblestone effects in porch-facing and chimney are employed in this cozy five-room bungalow of the most accepted type. The stone enclosure of the porch capped with cement, forms a wide ledge with a couple of steps alongside the pillars for flowers and plants. The arch extending between the corner pillars in a single span gives an open effect to the porch and provides space for light from without and view from within. This is appreciated in the big living room. The window seat at one end and the fireplace at the other serves to make this the most inviting room in the house. This large room adapts itself to the most effective style of finish and furnishings. The dining room is second only to this spacious room in point of attractiveness and utility. A small hallway enables one to reach the bath room from the bed rooms, kitchen or dining room without passing through the other chambers.

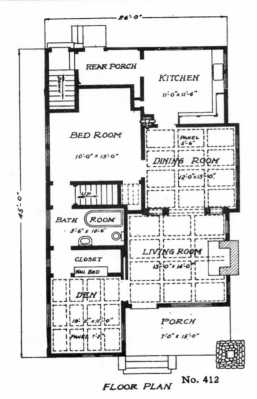

FLOOR PLAN   No. 412

Estimated cost..............................$4000.00
Price of plans as shown or reversed   15.00

412—In every way this is a typical Craftsman bungalow. Wide, overhanging eaves and extra heavy verge board make it very substantial in appearance. Cobblestones for the large single porch column add a pleasing touch to the otherwise plain exterior. The use of pressed brick with cobblestones laid in a vine design makes this massive fireplace very unique. The exterior is of sawed cedar shakes stained silver gray, which harmonizes with the white trim of the smooth woodwork and gray cobblestone. The roof, though low, has cross gables and is plenty high enough for a couple of small chambers and sleeping porch in the upper story. Opening from the living room through a single sliding door is a den, with a built-in wall bed, so arranged that it can be used for a bed room in case of an emergency. The bed room is larger than is ordinarily found in a bungalow. It has two windows and an alcove on one side, just large enough for a bed. Leading from the kitchen is a latticed porch, which can be used as a breakfast room.

Our plans are practical.

Hints on Bungalow Building—Pointers

Build a house which will sell readily. An attractive house will command a better price by several hundred dollars than the common kind, and it costs no more.

Use the best shingles on your roof; it is false economy to use a cheap grade of roofing. Your roof should be as simple as possible; every valley means a weak place that might leak.

Don't use cheap cement or mix it weak. This is not an item of heavy expense, but a very important one.

Closets should be put in wherever you can find available space. Cut down the size of rooms if necessary.

Use plenty of windows. Glass is cheaper than lumber. Be sure and have the kitchen with sink right under a window.

Have your fireplace built right. Avoid smoke and excessive discomfort by having it built according to our detail plans.

Don't build a bath room without outside windows or located so that it cannot be reached without going through a bed room or kitchen. (This is a fault with many small cottages and apartments that can just as well be avoided.)

A clothes chute in the bath room is mighty handy; it can be arranged with a seat on either side and a locker under.

Gained by years *of* Actual Experience

Care should be used in arranging the position of your windows and doors. By all means place windows so that a draft may be had from any direction to air rooms. Consider the position of beds and other large pieces of furniture. Bed room windows should give good light to your dressing table.

Arrange your kitchen to prevent extra steps. Don't build an old style pass-pantry when you can have a neat, compact, buffet kitchen such as we put in our bungalows.

Use good hardware on your front door and a good lock on your back door, even if you have to use cheap locks on inside doors.

A cooling closet is a necessity, and should be ventilated from an outside wall.

Don't let your carpenter fool you into starting without detail plans. He can not execute the work as well without them, and the best he can do is to make a patched-up job that resembles the design. More than that, he has everything his own way. He may say that he will do this or that, but there are a hundred things, probably far more important, of which he will say nothing, but which deeply concern you, and these are things for which you may have to pay a fancy extra price when they should have been included in the original contract. Don't be penny wise and pound foolish. You may save money in the beginning, but in the end lose several hundred dollars on account of not having a complete set of plans and specifications.

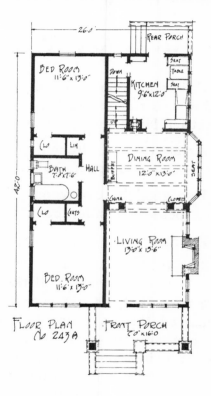

FLOOR PLAN
No 243 A

243-A—Almost like a palatial cottage is the exterior of this bungalow, with its irregular lines of roof taking away the small, uniform appearance found in many bungalows. Designed for a deep, narrow lot, the rooms are all carefully proportioned, more attention being paid to closet space than is usual in small homes. Shelves are provided in both of the large closets, as well as in the large linen closet. A Pullman diner is provided in the kitchen. The bed rooms are at either corner of the house, with hall connecting and bath room between. The living room off the substantial-looking porch has coved ceiling and artistic entrance to the dining room. The latter has an immense bay jutting out from the side of the wall, with six lights and a ledge within for flowers, or if preferred for a window seat.

Estimated cost..$4000.00
Price of plans as shown or reversed   15.00

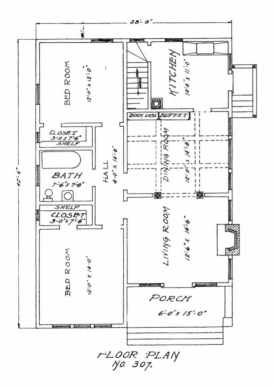

FLOOR PLAN
No. 307.

Estimated cost.........................$4000.00
Price of plans as shown or reversed   15.00

307—Giving a foothold for all manner of climbing vine, the clinker brick chimney and porch columns of this bungalow provide a touch of nature which relieves the otherwise severe lines of the place. A broad, deep porch sets into the front of the house and leads into a good-sized living room, with fireplace on the outer wall. Passing through the wide opening, one enters the dining room, where the eye is immediately struck by the appearance of size and features of the finish. A dark-green stain for all the woodwork, with a light burlap or Japanese paper on the walls between narrow panel strips, has been employed in the finish of this room with the best of results. The housewife is impressed by the large bed room closets—more than seven feet deep with a wide shelf along the side.

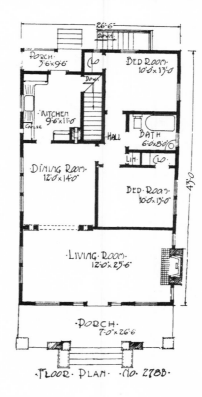

·FLOOR· PLAN· ·No· 278b·

278-B—Many original ideas are apparent in this bungalow, more on the exterior than within, which follows one of the most satisfactory designs. The curved arch of the cozy little porch entrance and the concrete columns passing through the roof and slightly curved at the ends are the first distinctive parts to impress the observer. The front door is largely of glass, with diamond-shaped panes of large size. The windows beside it are long and narrow and also have the diamond pane, as do the upper sashes of the front and side windows. The living room extends across the full width of the house and gets the light from the wide windows on either side of the door, and from the door itself. There is a small porch off the kitchen. Note the compact arrangement of the bedroom closets and cellar stairway.

Estimated cost..............................$3900.00
Price of plans as shown or reversed   15.00

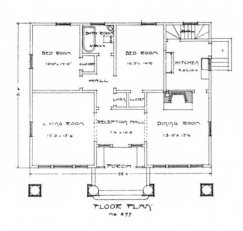

FLOOR PLAN
no 277

277—A snappy design, this, with the four large columns of the porch and double pergola suggesting in miniature the imposing colonial or southern mansion. While adding dignity, these columns do not detract from the cozy appearance of the bungalow. This is enhanced by the broad seats at either side of the wide entrance. The artistic merit of the pillars is doubled by their graduated base and cap blocks. A dainty little reception hall is found after passing through the door with the living room on one hand and the dining room on the other. The fireplace is in the dining room, necessitating only one chimney for the mantel and the kitchen range as well. The bath room can be reached from any room in the house except the kitchen without passing through another room.

Estimated cost............................$3900.00
Price of plans as shown or reversed   15.00

Estimated cost....$3900.00
Price of plans as
shown or re-
versed 15.00

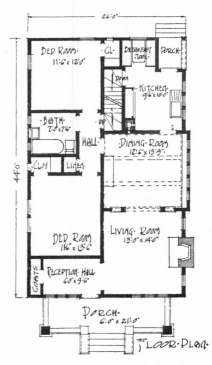

No. 247-A

247-A—The use of brick and cement for the foundation and upper story, respectively, with siding sandwiched in, makes the outside of the house very pleasing in appearance.   The porch extends nearly across the front of the house and has a large square timber for a support at either corner.   The braces protrude through the verge board rather than appearing beneath it.   Entering the living room from the porch, one finds the mantel on the outer wall, affording opportunity for an attractive chimney of rough brick without. There is a broad arch leading to the dining room, which is beamed and has a square window at the side with seat beneath.   Back of the kitchen is a good-sized porch and a pretty built-in breakfast nook.   A hall connects the bed rooms with the dining room and bath room.

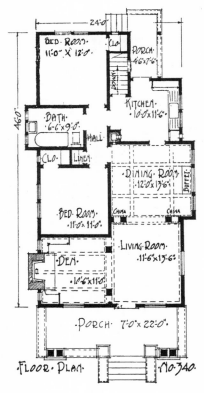

·FLOOR· PLAN· No·340·

Estimated cost.................................$3800.00

Price of plans as shown or reversed   15.00

340—The heavy brick work of porch walls and piers is probably the predominant feature. The large cement urns which are an integral part of the masonry work, providing novel plant holders, are rather unusual. Next to the brickwork, the effective treatment of porch soffit and the repeated vertical lines of the porch gable help take this house out of the ordinary class. The brackets supporting the verge boards show an interesting bit of band saw art. The floor plan is a marvel of compactness and utility, providing six fine rooms of the maximum size possible in the ground space, 24 feet by 46 feet, with the minimum amount of space devoted to hall. The den is a very attractive room, with cleverly designed fireplace, a seat and bookcases. The dining room has china closets and a buffet. The kitchen shows a good arrangement of cabinets.

One need not necessarily be rich to give grace and charm to his habitation.—Wagner.

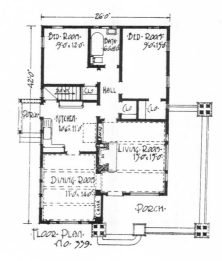

339—Rather unique in treatment, the long lines of verge and ridge, the different porch rail and the massive 8x8-inch brackets and lookouts, lend a distinction seldom seen in a home of like size and cost. The porch floor and steps are cement while the corner piers of the porch are shingled. The space under the roof is ventilated by providing a small gable dormer with latticed wall. Special care was taken in designing the rooms which go to make up this splendid five-room plan. Designing is the correct word—mere planning would never produce the results shown—each room is complete. No guess work here, not an unnecessary line drawn and not a line left out which would be needed to provide comfort and beauty. Economy is also thought of, one chimney serves every need.

Estimated cost...................................$3800.00

Price of plans as shown or reversed   15.00

Use plenty of windows; glass is cheaper than lumber.

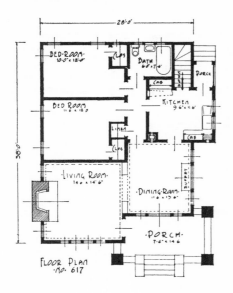

FLOOR PLAN
NO. 617

Estimated cost..............................$3700.00

Price of plans as shown or reversed   15.00

617—This bungalow, built in the midst of a row of bungalows, is easily the most successful in plan and design of the entire row. The exterior—the repeating lines of the heavy piers of the porch, its brick capped wall providing fine supports for additional flower boxes and the exceptional treatment of the roof lines—had a great deal to do with the success of the design. The designer had a lucky day when he schemed out this plan, for he has in a space twenty-eight by thirty-eight obtained five of the largest and best arranged rooms we have ever seen. Every room is well lighted with the windows so placed that they do not interfere with the placing of furniture to the best advantage.

Our plans include details of interior finish.

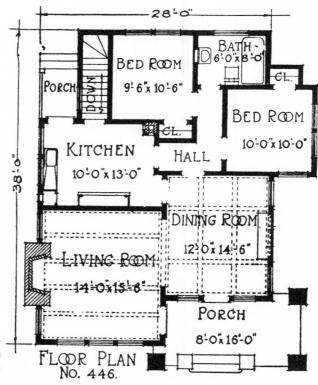

28'-0"

38'-0"

PORCH

BED ROOM
9'-6" x 10'-6"

BATH·
6'-0" x 8'-0"

CL.

DOWN

KITCHEN
10'-0" x 13'-0"

CL.

HALL

BED ROOM
10'-0" x 10'-0"

DINING ROOM
12'-0" x 14'-6"

LIVING ROOM
14'-0" x 15'-6"

PORCH
8'-0" x 16'-0"

FLOOR PLAN
No. 446.

446—With five rooms on one floor, this bungalow is one of the most attractive designs we show in this book. It is laid out in the most simple manner possible, with the living room occupying the entire front. The living and dining rooms have oak floors, paneled walls and beam ceilings. There is an unusual arrangement of the bed room hall, removing the former from any noise in the rest of the house. The kitchen is of good size and convenient. In addition to the regular fixtures, it has a large built-in ventilated cooler. This house has a more graceful and finished appearance than many of the rustic bungalows.

Estimated cost................................$3700.00
Price of plans as shown or reversed   15.00

Don't build an old-style cottage.

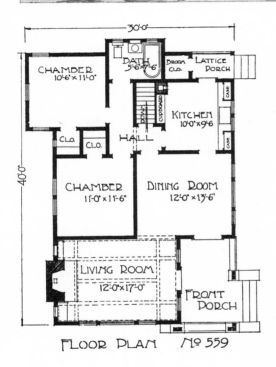

FLOOR PLAN No 559

Estimated cost..........................$3700.00

Price of plans as shown or reversed   15.00

559—Five good rooms arranged in a very compact plan.   The exterior is of wide and narrow boards alternate.   The porch walls and buttresses of clinker brick are fine bits of design, and are built to last forever.   The living room has beam ceiling.   The fireplace is at the end opposite the entrance door flanked on one side with a seat and on the other by a neat bookcase.   Both the bed rooms are convenient to the bath room and each room is provided with a roomy closet.

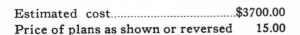

No. 446-A—SEVERAL GABLES MAKE IT AN INTERESTING HOME

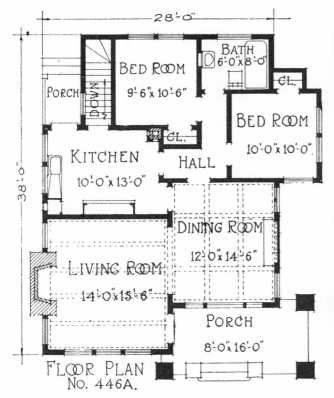

FLOOR PLAN No. 446A.

28'-0"

BED ROOM 9'-6" x 10'-6"

BATH 6'-0" x 8'-0"

PORCH

DOWN

CL.

BED ROOM 10'-0" x 10'-0"

KITCHEN 10'-0" x 13'-0"

HALL

CL.

38'-0"

DINING ROOM 12'-0" x 14'-6"

LIVING ROOM 14'-0" x 15'-6"

PORCH 8'-0" x 16'-0"

Estimated cost............................$3700.00
Price of plans as shown or reversed   15.00

446-A—Very similar in plan and general lines to No. 446 but providing a shingle roof for those who cannot approve of the patent roofing. It is neat and inexpensive and one of the most useful of bungalow plans. The entire porch is finished in stucco while the house proper is siding to the heavy watertable and shingles above. The fireplace wall of the living room is utilized to the full, having leaded glass bookcases on either side and ornate high sash above.

The planning of a bungalow home is an art.

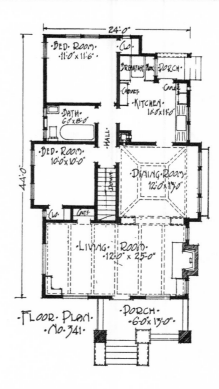

·FLOOR·PLAN·
·NO·341·

341—Stone properly used can help wonderfully in the attractiveness of a house design. This bungalow has its porch work and chimney of the rough cut sandstone laid up in black cement mortar and the use of this material has given the house the necessary touch of light to set off the rather dark stain of the re-sawed cedar siding. Flower boxes enhance the beauty of the design. The floor plan illustrates an especially good arrangement, two of the best parts being the large living room, 12 feet by 23 feet, with fireplace, seat and bookcases, and the attractive Pullman diner off the kitchen. Two other features about this house which are rather unusual in a bungalow of this size are the coat closet off the front room and the location of the basement stairway which is so placed that if an attic is to be finished at any time, a stairway can be installed without disturbing the ground floor plan.

Estimated cost...$3700.00
Price of plans as shown or reversed   15.00

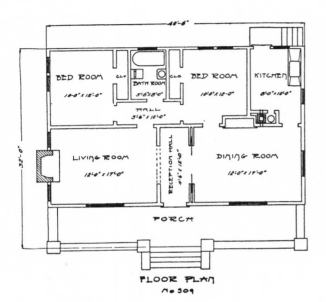

FLOOR PLAN
No 309

Estimated cost..$3600.00
Price of plans as shown or reversed   10.00

309—Search far and wide and it would be hard to find a better looking or more satisfactory bungalow than this for two or three people.   Rough brick for the large outside chimney and the four porch columns add a pleasing touch to the otherwise plain exterior. The living room is at the left on entering the reception hall and the dining room on the right, the former having a wide entrance with pillars and arch and the latter arranged with sliding doors, so that after the meal is over the servant can do the work without being in view of guests or household.   The door between the kitchen and dining room is at the extreme side.

Convenience in our plans is our main object.

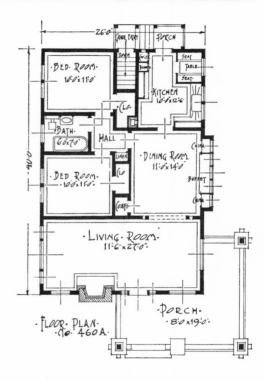

·FLOOR· PLAN·
·co· 460 A·

460-A—The exterior of this beautiful home is a strikingly attractive combination of vari-colored cobblestones for the walls of the porch and the fireplace, shingled walls and heavy brackets. The shingles are almost the natural color with light brown stain, and the trimmings are painted a very dark brown. Cobblestones properly selected and laid up are very artistic, but the use of native materials like any other good thing can be easily over-worked. One must have a good understanding of the "eternal fitness of things" or a rustic effect among things of another style will look out of place. The living room is large and well lighted, connecting to the dining room by a large arch. The dining room is paneled and ceiling beamed and the extra large built-in buffet directly opposite the square bay window adds a pleasing touch to this attractive room.

Estimated cost...$3600.00
Price of plans as shown or reversed   10.00

Have your fireplace built right—see our plans.

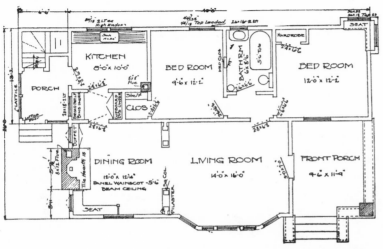

Floor Plan No. 400

400—In every way this is a characteristic bungalow. It has the wide, overhanging roof and rafter ends exposed. The design is an original one, presenting a broad front to the street. The porch wall and column and the outside of the fireplace are laid up with cobblestones, which look especially well in a design like this. The dimensions are twenty-six by forty feet, not including the rear porch. Every possible convenience is provided for all rooms. The arch between the front rooms contains built-in bookcases with adjustable shelves. The dining room fireplace has a tile face. On one side is a lounging seat and on the other a low buffet with casement windows above. The pantry cupboard and work shelf have paneled doors, drawers and bins. The kitchen and bath room have an enameled plaster finish to a height of five feet in imitation white tile. The house is well finished throughout and answers in every detail the requirements of a small family.

Estimated cost.................................$3600.00
Price of plans as shown or reversed   10.00

A small kitchen with well planned cupboards saves steps.

331—ALL WHO PASS THE BUNGALOW NOTE IT IS VERY REFRESHING

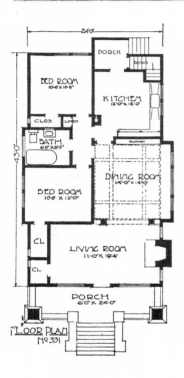

Estimated cost............................$3600.00
Price of plans as shown or reversed   10.00

331—Cobblestones and shingles.   Five rooms and a bath.   Here is a living room with a fine fireplace and a coat and hat closet and with two great windows in its front wall.   Here, too, is a very good dining room fourteen feet by fourteen feet, a kitchen twelve by twelve with full equipment of sink, cupboards, cooler and bins, a couple of bed rooms with great closets, a large bath room hall with linen closet and a very good bath room withal.   There is also a fine basement with concrete floor and walls and fine lighting.

Our plans are revelations in the utilization of space.

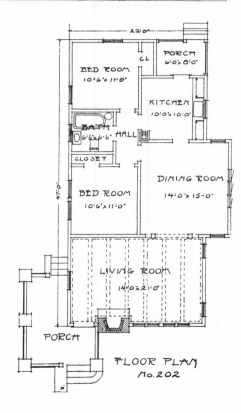

FLOOR PLAN
No. 202

202—Two features are at once apparent in this roomy bungalow. First the porch at the corner lending distinction to the exterior as well as providing a wealth of space for outdoor life. Second, the living room extending across the entire front of the house and nearly 15 feet in width. Thought of bright summer days and balmy moonlight nights are inspired by the attractive porch, with the substantial brick pillars matching the broad brick chimney, its wide eaves and commodious size both on the front and side of the house. No more pleasant spot could be found on hot days than this porch with broad, inviting hammocks, pillowed seats and lounging chairs, distributed among potted flowers and palms and other green plants. And when cooler weather prevails, the spacious living room with a roaring fire in the huge open fireplace satisfies every home instinct. The room has a heavy beam ceiling and is as light as it is large. The dining room is also a large and cheery place with windows on three sides.

Estimated cost...$3600.00
Price of plans as shown or reversed   10.00

A good home is a debt every man owes his wife.

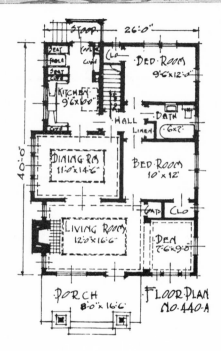

Estimated cost...$3600.00
Price of plans as shown or reversed   10.00

440 A—A very pleasing bungalow is shown in this view. The porch, with its low cement floor and pyramid-shaped pedestals of stucco, is perhaps the most attractive feature of the exterior. The outer walls of the house as high as the water-table are covered with cedar siding, with shingles above. The interior may be considered a model plan. The six rooms are very conveniently arranged and are of good size. Note the large living room with an open fireplace at one end. The large window in front is plate glass. If you are lucky enough to be the owner of a building site with a view, by all means use plate glass if possible, and so gain a wonderful picture for your walls which would be lost if common glass was used. This is a very popular design.

In building use the best materials. Cheap ones cost more in the end.

PAGE SEVENTY-SEVEN

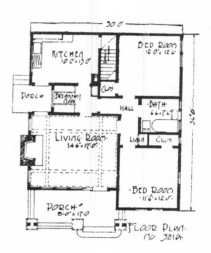

321-A—This is one of our most popular low priced bungalows and has the appearance of costing several hundred dollars more than it really does. Avoiding a stuffy vestibule, entrance is made directly into the living room. The house has only four rooms, but all are of good size and provide ample space for a small family. The more the plan is studied, the more one appreciates the conveniences of this compact little home. The house has a concrete basement under the rear half. The siding is of 6 and 12-inch rustic boards, laid alternately.

Estimated cost..............................$3500.00

Price of plans as shown or reversed   10.00

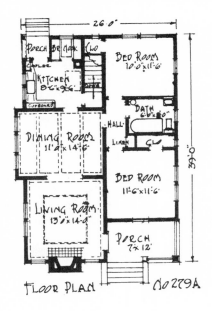

FLOOR PLAN   No 279 A

Estimated cost..................................$3500.00
Price of plans as shown or reversed   10.00

279 A—Something totally different is found in the combined cobblestone and brick chimney which forms such an important item in the exterior of this home. A base of large cobblestones supports the chimney with varied designs in stone, covering part of the brick work even to the top, which carries a cement cap. Very plain and solid are the braces which support the overhanging roof. In fact, the chimney is the only digression from the dignified simplicity of the entire exterior. Within it is different. The living room has an attractive brick mantel, while the French doors opening into the dining room affords privacy for the dinner party. The bed room arrangement is excellent. The dining room bay is the full length of the whole room, giving space for a little greenery or other flowery nook and adding much to the enjoyment of the daily meals.

Does it pay to take chances?

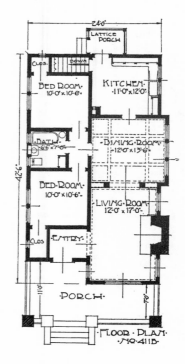

411-B—Five rooms arranged in the most approved manner with a reception hall additional. Rough cedar siding is used for the body of the house and the porch columns are of selected clinker brick. The verge boards are especially heavy, being in one piece three inches thick and fourteen inches wide. The lifting of the gable points is a fine suggestion. Details are included with the plans for fireplace, the china closets in the buttresses between living and dining rooms and the full kitchen equipment.

Estimated cost..................................$3500.00
Price of plans as shown or reversed   10.00

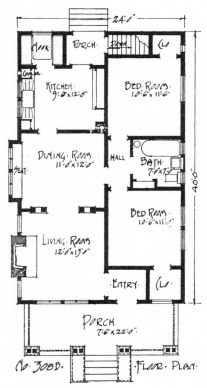

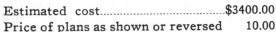

Estimated cost...............................$3400.00
Price of plans as shown or reversed   10.00

308-B—This house is built on rather severe lines, but the combination of the brick porchwork, with heavy chains connecting the posts, and square timbers running to the edge of the roof, makes an excellent impression. The front of the house below the gable as far as the porch is of plaster with a small amount of paneling. The balance of the house to the masonry work is siding. The interior includes a vestibule which is practically part of the living room, so hospitable is the doorway between, but which is apart sufficiently to keep the dirt and litter from the main room. The mantel is of pressed brick, the dark and light tones alternating. The dining room has a big window seat. The kitchen is well provided with cupboards and a neat Pullman breakfast nook is in an alcove at the rear. The bed rooms are connected by a hall leading past the bath room.

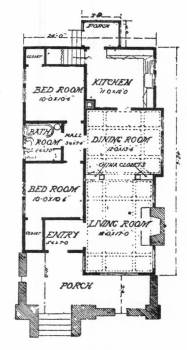

Floor Plan No. 411

411—This bungalow is entirely new and original in design. The exterior is composed of several very ordinary elements, so that the builder secures an extraordinary bungalow at an exceedingly low cost. The use of clinker brick and resawed cedar siding makes this bungalow very pleasing in appearance. The porch floor is cement, as are also the wide steps. The interior is just as pleasing in appearance as the exterior. A small entry leads to the living room, which has a fireplace on the outer wall, affording a foothold for clinging vines without. The arch between the living room and dining room contains two built-in china closets with adjustable shelves. The kitchen is just the right size, with cabinets on two sides, with sink beneath the window, affording a flood of light. The basement stairs lead from kitchen, which is an important item in cold weather.

Estimated cost..$3400.00
Price of plans as shown or reversed   10.00

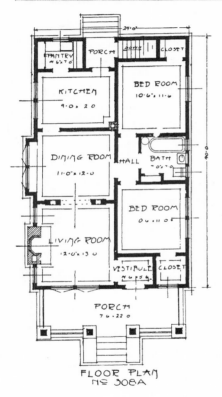

FLOOR PLAN
Nº 308A

Estimated cost................................$3400.00
Price of plans as shown or reversed   10.00

308-A—Similar in plan to Number 308-B on page seventy-nine, but in exterior so different. The porch treatment, the spreading pedestals of clinker brick and the heavy columns surmounting same are just the right size. The smooth siding on the walls is right, rough siding on this would have spoiled the effect. We have tried again and again but we have never yet conceived a plan arrangement as acceptable to as many people as this has been.

Place the kitchen sink under a window if possible.

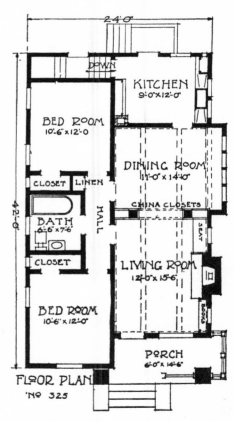

KITCHEN
9'-0" x 12'-0"

BED ROOM
10'-6" x 12'-0

DINING ROOM
11'-0" x 14'-0"

CLOSET LINEN

CHINA CLOSETS

BATH
6'-6" x 7'-6"

HALL

CLOSET

LIVING ROOM
12'-0" x 15'-6"

BED ROOM
10'-6" x 12'-0"

PORCH
6'-0" x 14'-6"

FLOOR PLAN
Nº 325

325—This attractive bungalow is an interesting study in plan and design on account of its direct style. Note the manner in which every available bit of space is utilized. The porch columns are finished in the popular cement stucco. The exterior is shingled and is stained a silver gray, which forms a pleasing contrast with the white trim of the smooth woodwork. We recommend this design. Estimated cost................................$3400.00 Price of plans as shown or reversed 10.00

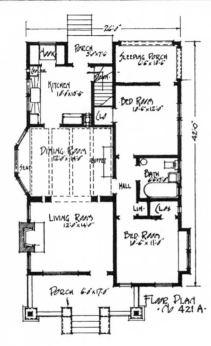

Estimated cost......................................$3400.00
Price of plans as shown or reversed   10.00

421-A—This bungalow, though not large, possesses pleasing characteristics. The walls are covered with rough cedar siding, stained a dark brown, and the casings, brackets, and posts are trimmed in white. The five rooms afford sufficient accommodations for a medium-sized family, and the finish is such that the occupant can be proud of his home. The rooms are large, and better laid out than the average bungalow, also having more of the modern conveniences. The arch between the dining and living rooms is designed for service as well as for looks, containing a bookcase having adjustable shelves. The top of the bookcase is $5\frac{1}{2}$ feet high and carries heavy, square pillars which support an arch between the rooms. The screened sleeping porch is large enough for a full sized bed.

FLOOR PLAN
No. 439A.

439-A—Overhanging eaves, a wide verge board, with heavy exposed rafter ends make the exterior of this bungalow unique and cozy in appearance. The entrance leads directly into the living room, which is divided from the dining room by a wide, open arch. The interior is arranged along the best bungalow lines. A small hallway leads from the dining room to the front bed room and bath. The kitchen has a built-in cabinet and a stairway leading to the basement. The basement is 20x26 and has a concrete floor.

Estimated cost...$3300.00
Price of plans as shown or reversed   10.00

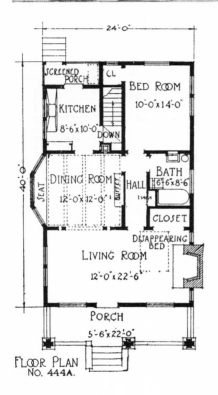

FLOOR PLAN
NO. 444A.

Estimated cost..................................$3300.00
Price of plans as shown or reversed   10.00

444-A—A sensible bungalow design with a standard four-room plan. The living room occupies the entire front of the house and is equipped with a disappearing bed. The dining room has a bay window with seat beneath. Take notice of the manner in which every bit of available space is utilized, as shown by the closet arrangement for bed rooms and the handy linen closet. The bath can be reach from any room in the house, except the kitchen, without passing through another room. The bed room, ten feet wide and fourteen feet long, is planned to provide several good arrangements for furniture.

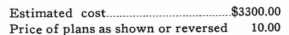

A good home is a debt every man owes to his wife.

FLOOR PLAN No 742.

742—Here is another popular plan of five rooms. Note the large size of the rooms and convenience of arrangement. The exterior is covered with rough six-inch lap cedar siding, and the trim is of surfaced fir. The floors in all rooms are of number one fir and the finish is slash grain fir stained in living and dining room. Bathroom and bedrooms are in white enamel. Ample cupboard space is provided in the kitchen, assuring plenty of storage for provisions and utensils. The design of the large fireplace is one that assures a maximum of heat in the room with no smoke. The details show a mantel that looks fine in burlap brick. It is truly the heart of the home.

Estimated cost............................$3200.00
Price of plans as shown or reversed   10.00

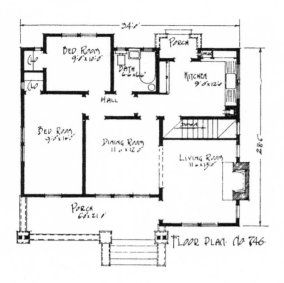

FLOOR PLAN No. 746.

746—A snug and cozy little home of five rooms requiring a lot not less than forty feet wide. The front porch nestling under the sloping roof, 6'-0" wide and 21'-0" long, is fine. The outside walls are covered with rough siding to the watertable and red cedar shingles laid alternate wide and narrow courses to the weather above. The rooms are so arranged that three have an outlook to the front, which makes the plan especially desirable for a lot having a good view in this direction. The bathroom has the Craftsman feature of medicine case with mirror door between two windows. The living room has a very pretty fireplace of burlap brick.

Estimated cost..........................$3200.00
Price of plans as shown or reversed   10.00

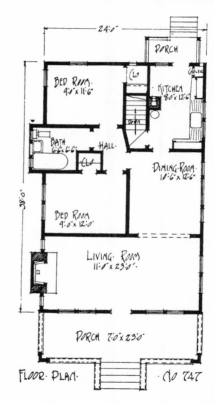

FLOOR PLAN. No 747

747—We do not hesitate to say that the plan shown here will fill the requirements of a great number of prospective home builders and prove to be one of our most popular designs, as we have combined in it an exterior similar to that of the most popular home we ever put out, and a floor plan that cannot be excelled in the ground space the same size or for the expenditure of a like amount of money. The large living room with its attractive fireplace of brick and the grouping of the remaining rooms about the hall are the features we know will appeal to all. We would suggest that those interested in this design study also those shown on pages 20 and 21 before making their decision.

Estimated cost..............................$3200.00

Price of plans as shown or reversed   10.00

Building to sell? Our bungalows are ready sellers.

PAGE NINETY

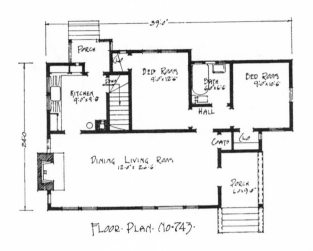

FLOOR PLAN No. 743.

Estimated cost.................................$3200.00
Price of plans as shown or reversed   10.00

743—This neat little bungalow has a substantial appearance not very often found in a house that costs as little as this one. The combination dining room and living room occupies practically the entire front, sharing the honor only with the porch, which is 6'-0" by 9'-0". The fireplace is at the opposite end of the room and in plain view from the front door, extending a prompt and cheerful welcome to all comers. There is a coat closet for the wraps and the other closets are so placed that they do not take up any extra space, and at the same time are provided with windows for light and ventilation. The kitchen is well arranged.

Have your bed rooms finished in light colors.

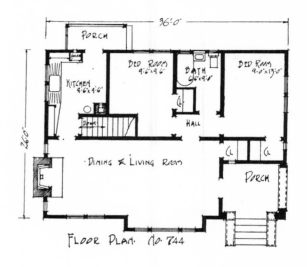

FLOOR PLAN No. 744

744—The exterior design is simple but artistic and so composed of several very ordinary elements that the builder secures a very good looking bungalow at an extremely low cost. Washington red cedar shingles laid in courses alternating wide and narrow are used above the watertable, while six-inch rough cedar siding acts as the skirting below. The plan is very similar to that on the preceding page. The living room is 11'-6" x 25'-6", not including the bay window. The bedrooms are both of good size and each is supplied with a large closet. The kitchen plan is one of the best.

Estimated cost....................................$3200.00

Price of plans as shown or reversed   10.00

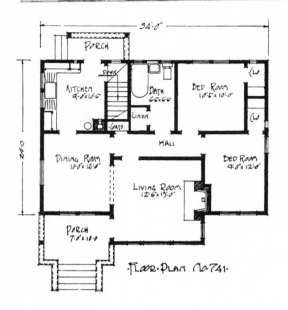

FLOOR PLAN No. 741

PORCH

KITCHEN 9'-0" x 10'-6"

BATH 6'-6" x 6'-6"

BED ROOM 10'-6" x 10'-0"

DOWN

LINEN

COATS

HALL

DINING ROOM 10'-0" x 12'-0"

BED ROOM 9'-0" x 12'-0"

LIVING ROOM 12'-6" x 13'-0"

PORCH 7'-0" x 18'-0"

34'-0"

741—The thatched roof English farm house furnished the design for this fine little home of five rooms. The walls are of four-inch cedar lap siding and the roof is shingled. The porch is at the corner with the entrance door at the side of the living room. The dining room directly back of the porch is conveniently located in regard to kitchen and hall. More than the usual number of closets are provided, including besides the regular bedroom closets a place for linen and one for wraps. The basement stair is well arranged both for interior and exterior use. A lot not less than forty feet, and the wider the better, is required for this bungalow.

Estimated cost..................................$3200.00
Price of plans as shown or reversed   10.00

The fireplace is the center of the home—built it right.

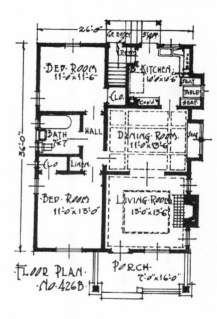

FLOOR PLAN
No. 426B

426 B—Here is a novel little home—quite on the rustic style. While the exterior is quite modest, the use of dimension shingles, laid with care and an eye to the unusual, produces an out-of-the-ordinary effect, which is supplemented by the white stucco of porch pedestals and chimney. The general arrangement of rooms is unbeatable. The utmost possible use is made of every inch of space provided, especially so in the kitchen where in a floor area ten feet by ten feet, six inches, are provided two cupboards, a cooler, location for range where it receives good light and a dandy pullman diner or breakfast nook. The stairway to basement has been so contrived that it serves also as a grade entry to basement which is a great convenience in wet weather.

Estimated cost.................................$3200.00
Price of plans as shown or reversed   10.00

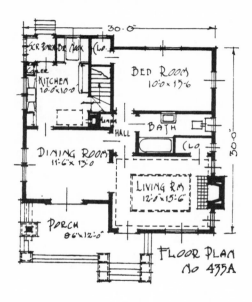

FLOOR PLAN No 435A

Estimated cost..............................$3100.00

Price of plans as shown or reversed   10.00

435 A—Paving brick and shingles are used in the construction of this house. The porch is only partially covered, the entrance door being sheltered by a neat hood supported on brackets, and the floor and steps are of cement. The plan calls for four rooms and bath. They are well arranged with a pass hall in the exact center. The living room is provided with a roomy closet, in which, if the occupant of the home so desires, can be placed a "In-a-door" bed, by means of which the living room can be converted into a bed room if the necessity arises. French doors separate the dining room from the living room and a double-acting door leads into the kitchen where we find all the needed cupboards and the much-prized breakfast nook.

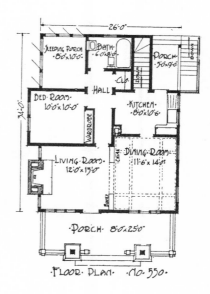

·FLOOR·PLAN· ·NO·550·

550—A ground space 26 feet by 34 feet has seldom produced a better four-room arrangement than is here illustrated. The exterior is one that has never failed to call out favorable comment. The cement stuccoed skirting contrasts well with the stained shingles and woodwork. The four rooms are so grouped around the pass hall that one can readily reach any room in the house, except the dining room without passing through any other room. The kitchen is well provided with cabinet space and china closet and book cases are built in the buttresses of the dining room and living room arch. The old-fashioned closet in the bedroom has given way to the up-to-date wardrobe where the articles you want are not covered up by a dozen that you do not want. The splendid sleeping porch is worthy of mention—all the fresh air that you can possibly desire is yours.

Estimated cost..................................$3100.00
Price of plans as shown or reversed   10.00

Our plans are a little better than seems necessary.

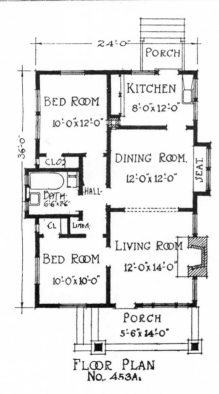

FLOOR PLAN
No. 453A.

24'-0"

PORCH

KITCHEN
8'-0"x12'-0"

BED ROOM
10'-0"x12'-0"

36'-0"

CLO.

BATH
6'-6"x7'-6"

HALL

DINING ROOM.
12'-0"x12'-0"

SEAT

CL. LINEN

BED ROOM
10'-0"x10'-0"

LIVING ROOM
12'-0"x14'-0"

PORCH
5'-6"x14'-0"

Estimated cost.................................$3000.00
Price of plans as shown or reversed   10.00

453-A—The easy sloping roof and double gables give this design the hospitable appearance so much desired in the home exterior. By the use of several very ordinary elements, the builder is able to construct a house at a cost that is far less than one would think at a first glance. The porch foundation, pedestals and railing are cement blocks, and the fireplace is built of clinker brick pointed up with black mortar. The interior is a standard, five-room plan and is used more than any plan shown in this book.

No. 456-A—THE CEMENT STUCCO BELOW THE WATERTABLE IS A PLEASING BIT OF DESIGN

456-A—This has proved to be a very popular plan on account of its porch treatment. The four rooms are arranged to get the largest amount of room and provide for a screened porch in the rear. The exterior walls below the watertable and the porch pedestals are cement stucco on metal lath. Above this the walls are cedar shingles laid six inches to the weather about one inch apart. The head casing of the windows is carried around the house as a belt course.

FLOOR PLAN
No. 456A

456-B—A five-room plan, twenty-four feet by thirty-six feet, with a cement floored basement under the rear half of the building. In exterior appearance the same as 456-A, and also the same in construction and finish, except that the front porch and steps are wood instead of cement. The rooms are all of good size and are well arranged, every bit of space being utilized. The screened porch is large and provides a splendid place for the refrigerator.

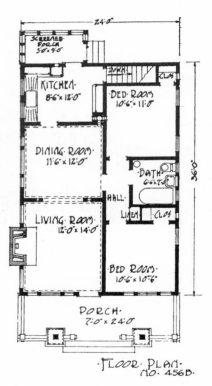

FLOOR PLAN
NO. 456B.

Estimated cost No. 456 A.................$2700.00
Estimated cost No. 456B...................$3000.00
Plans of either, as shown or reversed 10.00

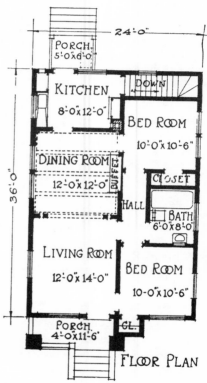

FLOOR PLAN

428—This plan offers an inexpensive home with the necessities of a five-room bunga-low 24x36 on the ground and well adapted to a narrow lot. The treatment of the gables in front is very attractive. The whole exterior is covered with six-inch rough cedar siding and stained a dark brown. The plan provides for a concrete basement 24 feet square with laundry trays.

Estimated cost................................$3000.00
Price of plans as shown or reversed   10.00

In building use best materials—cheap ones cost more in the end.

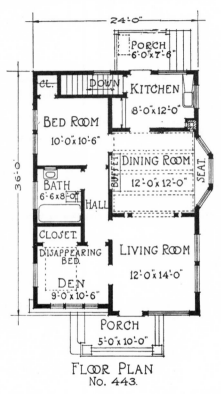

FLOOR PLAN
No. 443.

Estimated cost No. 456 B................$3000.00
Price of plans as shown or reversed   10.00

443—To the man that wants something different, we can submit this bungalow. The design has a touch of gingerbread work that so many want in a bungalow. The interior is well planned and provides a den, with a disappearing bed arranged so that it can be used as a chamber. A small hall makes the bath very accessible from any part of the house. The plan calls for a cement basement 24 feet square.

Our plans are practical.

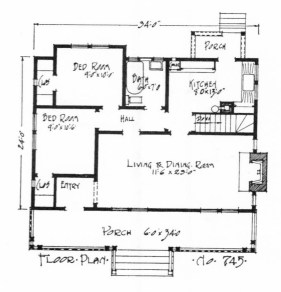

745—Another good arrangement with porch the full width of the front and six feet in depth. This certainly will hit some people in the right place if past experience in small house planning tells us anything. Not counting the porch, the ground area is 24 feet by 34 feet, and in it has been arranged four fine rooms, counting the great living room as one. A point in favor of this plan is the entry which protects the living room from the wet and dampness and provides a place for wraps. The exterior walls are covered with shingles laid six inches to the weather and stained above the watertable and rough siding, also stained, below.

Estimated cost..$2850.00
Price of plans as shown or reversed   10.00

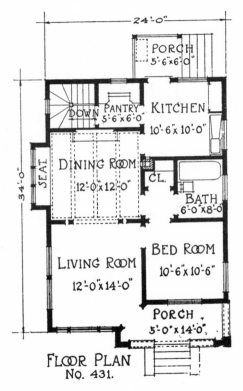

FLOOR PLAN
No. 431.

Estimated cost...........................$2850.00
Price of plans as shown or reversed   10.00

431—A charming little home that can be built on a lot as narrow as 30 feet. The outside construction is resawed siding and is stained a dark brown. Note the handy arrangement of the floor plan in every bit of available space being used. Avoiding a stuffy vestibule, the entrance leads directly into the living room. The happy part of the interior is the dining room, which has beam ceiling, panel wainscoting, and a beautiful built-in buffet.

A cooling cabinet can be arranged in most any kitchen.

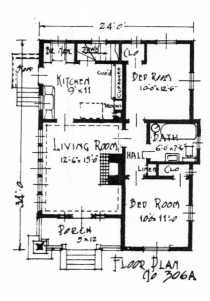

FLOOR PLAN No 306A

306 A—Realizing that the living room is the most important feature of the bungalow home, the designer has subverted the prominence of all the other rooms of this unique residence to emphasize that of the living room. Entered from a wide porch through a solid door flanked by high, narrow-leaded glass windows, this room is found to include dining apartment as well. A series of five windows on the side give ample light to and afford a view of the outside from every corner. The kitchen is tucked away in the rear, with the stairs leading to the basement in the kitchen corner, near the breakfast nook. The two bed rooms are connected by a hallway leading to the bath room and also having an opening into the living room. The exterior is worthy a few words, as the pyramid column of light brick supporting the porch roof at the corner forms practically the only unusual feature of the front.

Estimated cost..............................$2800.00

Price of plans as shown or reversed   10.00

FLOOR PLAN
No. 451A.

Estimated cost..............................$2400.00

Price of plans as shown or reversed   10.00

451-A—Here is a bungalow bargain that has been built many times by speculative builders everywhere. It contains many features that the home buyer wants and wherever built looks that it cost several hundred dollars more than it really did. The living room and dining room are of good size. Note the amount of closet space this little house provides. The exterior is beveled siding as high as the watertable with cedar shingles above. The plan does not provide for any inside stairway to the basement, but if desired one can easily be arranged to go where pantry is marked on plans.

Have your fireplace built right. See our plans.

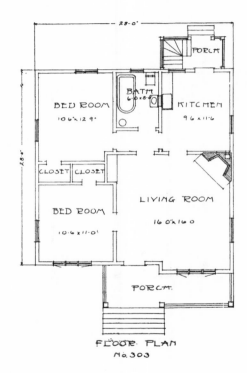

FLOOR PLAN
No. 303

303—A living room that embodies every idea of that term is a notable part of this cozy little bungalow. The room is 16 feet square and is a combined living and dining room. The corner opposite the stone or brick mantel is devoted to the buffet, fitting into the wall and leaving a wide expanse of room for the round mission table. This, when not in use for dining purposes, may be protected with a bit of drawn work or embroidered centerpiece, and with a fern dish or flower bowl will make a very attractive bit of the room furniture. A large corner bed room opens from the living room, while another door leads into the hall connecting the second bed chamber with the kitchen and bath room. A rear porch provides space for the ice chest and the entry to the basement.

Estimated cost..........................$2400.00
Price of plans as shown or reversed   10.00

Don't let over-confidence in your own ability spoil your bungalow.

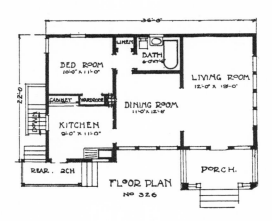

326—The photograph of this little bungalow shows what can be done for a small amount of money. While our estimates of cost will not apply in some parts of the East, the writer has just completed in Seattle, this cozy little home at the exact cost here estimated. For a small family we cannot recommend this design too strongly. Note the fact that in this plan you do not have to go through the bed room to get to the bath room from the dining room and that the door of the bath room is not directly opposite the dining room door. Note also the way the bed room wardrobe and the kitchen cabinet are dovetailed to save space.

Estimated cost................................$2400.00
Price of plans as shown or reversed   10.00

Our drawings are working plans.

· FLOOR PLAN · No. 455A ·

FLOOR PLAN · No 455B ·

455-A—Four rooms—living room, kitchen and two bedrooms, with bath in addition. Ample closet space is provided, and breakfast nook is conveniently located in kitchen. The outside is rather plain, six-inch rough siding, stained dark brown; but, when the grass and flowers are up, this home will present a very attractive picture. The front porch shown in cement, is a variation made by the builder from our plans, which call for a wood floor. Do not forget to order by number. This is 455-A.

Estimated cost......................................$2400.00
Price of plans as shown or reversed   10.00

455-B—A three-room detached apartment in a floor plan, twenty-four by twenty-four. For the young couple just starting housekeeping on a limited income, nothing could be better than to find an inexpensive lot and build this model plan. A moment's study will show its fine points. All the conveniences of an apartment with the privacy of a home, for less than you pay in rent for the apartment. The front porch is of wood. When ordering ask for number 455-B.

Estimated cost......................................$1700.00
Price of plans as shown or reversed   5.00

Our drawings are working plans.

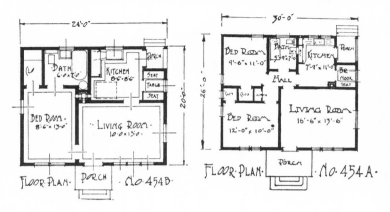

FLOOR PLAN - PORCH - No. 454 B

FLOOR PLAN - No. 454 A

Estimated cost..............................$1300.00

Price of plans as shown or reversed   5.00

454-B—Here's our baby—our smallest house. Isn't it a fine youngster—with the same economical arrangement of plumbing, and the even better placing of chimney in center of house, made possible because this is only a three-room plan. Not one inch is lost; in fact, some inches are doing the work of two. Don't delay building an hour, but order your plan Number 454-B this minute. The same statement regarding porch made for 454-A applies to 454-B.

454-A—A neat and attractive but not expensive exterior and a convenient four-room plan. Just study it a little while—can you plan a better arrangement in the space given? Note the economical placing of plumbing—the handy pass hall which connects every room in the house—the breakfast nook and roomy cabinets. Enough. You are writing your order now for number 454-A; but before we go, let us explain that the cement porch is a change from our plans, which call for wood framing throughout.

Estimated cost No. 456A..................$2,200.00

Price of plans as shown or reversed   5.00

Our plans are revelations in the utilization of space.

YOHO
SEATTLE

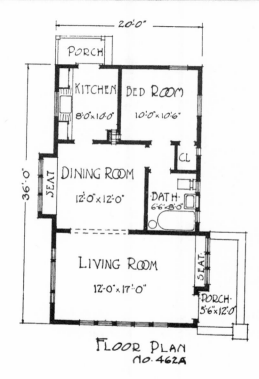

FLOOR PLAN
No. 462A

462-A—A half-timber effect, with lap siding substituted for the usual cement plaster in the panels, presenting a rather unique, but pretty, appearance. The plan is a convenient one—the builder gets the maximum amount of usefulness for the lowest possible cost. The four rooms are grouped about the central chimney in such a way that a stove can be placed in both dining room and bed room, as well as in the kitchen, thus assuring a warm home at all times. At a slight additional cost a fireplace can be built in the end of the living room, where the three windows are, that would add much to the homelike appearance of the room.

Estimated cost..$1700.00
Price of plans as shown or reversed..   5.00

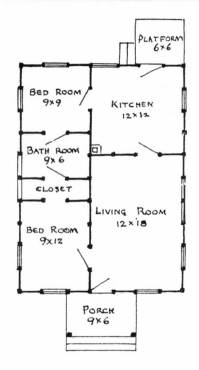

BUNGALOW "G", 21x30

This bungalow is very classy, complete and a big seller. Please note the large living room, bath room and closet space. This is intended for a portable house and as such is especially suitable as a summer camp or for use on a leased site. The estimated cost given is for the house without plumbing or plastering, which cannot be figured in the cost of a sectional dwelling.

Estimated cost................................$1000.00

Plans 5.00

FULL VALUE FOR YOUR MONEY

Our plans are practical working drawings, complete in every detail, and ready for any good carpenter, mason or builder to go ahead with the work. At the prices quoted, both for special and stock plans, we furnish two copies of complete blueprint plans, consisting of $\frac{1}{4}$-inch scale drawings of foundation, first and second floor plans (in two-story houses), four elevations and large scale details of all interior fixtures, such as fireplaces, arches, kitchen cabinets and other finish features. Typewritten specifications to supplement the drawings are enclosed to cover the general conditions of the contract, such as the excavation, masonry, carpentry, plastering, hardware, electrical work, plumbing, tinting, painting and other details.

SPECIAL PLANS: If you do not find a plan that meets your individual requirements, we will be glad to get up a special design for you, incorporating your own ideas. In this way you can get exactly what you want. It is our aim to give the people the best professional service at the lowest possible cost, and in this way make every customer a live advertiser. Our charges for special plans will be given on application.

In ordering special plans, kindly give the following information:

(1) Size and approximate grade of lot, also points of compass and direction of the most pleasant view.

(2) Nature of soil, depth and size of basement.

(3) Concrete, brick or stone foundation.

(4) Construction—frame, brick, stone or concrete.

(5) Number of rooms, and a rough sketch of the arrangement of same.

(6) Height of ceilings in basement and first floor.

(7) Kind of wood used in construction, as well as in the interior finish.

(8) Heating—hot air, steam or hot water.

(9) Fireplace and location of same.

(10) Inside trim, wainscoting, kitchen cupboards, buffet, beam ceilings, chair rail, art glass, china closets, etc.

TERMS: Our business is done strictly on a cash basis. No order will be filled unless accompanied by a remittance. This is an invariable rule and is made necessary on account of doing business in so many different parts of the country and is not meant as a reflection on your financial standing. These terms apply to everyone.

After the plans leave our office, we try to keep in touch with the builder and are glad to answer any inquiry or assist him in any way with our experience. Why? Because we want every bungalow built from our plans to prove a lasting advertisement for

Yours sincerely,

YOHO & MERRITT,

The Bungalow Craftsmen,
Seattle, U. S. A.

REFERENCES:
Metropolitan Bank, Seattle, Wash.
National City Bank, Seattle, Wash.
Bradstreet or Dun.